Penguin Books
The Shining Levels

John Wyatt is now Head Warden for the Lake District National Park, which involves him in a vast variety of duties over 866 square miles of Britain's largest national park. His father was a Lancashire cotton-mill overlooker and his mother was a Canadian of Scottish descent.

His first job was as a copy-boy at the Manchester office of the *Daily Telegraph* and since then he has had a multifarious career as a camp-site warden, forest worker, telegraphist in the Royal Navy, estate worker, sub-postmaster and North regional organizer for Oxfam.

John Wyatt

The Shining Levels

The Story of a Man Who Went Back to Nature

Drawings by Elisabeth Trimby

Penguin Books

Penguin Books Ltd, Harmondsworth,
Middlesex, England
Penguin Books, 625 Madison Avenue, New York,
New York 10022, U.S.A.
Penguin Books Australia Ltd,
Ringwood, Victoria, Australia
Penguin Books Canada Ltd, 2801 John Street,
Markham, Ontario, Canada L3R 1B4
Penguin Books (N.Z.) Ltd, 182–190 Wairau Road,
Auckland 10, New Zealand

First Published by Geoffrey Bles 1973
Published in Penguin Books 1976
Reprinted 1977, 1981

Copyright © John Wyatt, 1973
Illustrations copyright © Geoffrey Bles, 1973
All rights reserved

Set, printed and bound in Great Britain by
Cox & Wyman Ltd, Reading
Set in Linotype Pilgrim

Contents

1 *The Arrival*

I have been a countryman all my life. I have had a straw in my
mouth, a stick in my hand, and a dog at my heels almost from
the day I could walk. As a child this made me a peculiar misfit
because I was born and brought up in a Lancashire industrial
town within sight of a coal tip, within sound of a cotton mill,
and almost within smell of a black pudding and tripe factory.

But lemon-yellow charlock grew upon the tip. The poplar
hawk moths flew among the hen pens. The larks soared from
the fields beyond the allotments; and within fifteen minutes

walk there was a blessed wood. And I knew where the kingfisher flashed from the bank of its stream; and where the watervole nested, and the water-shrew trailed its pearl-bubbles. Beyond that there were the Pennine moors. Within a sixpenny bus ride there was the Peak District with its escarpments, pot holes, and gritstone crags, and I lived for long light evenings and the week-ends.

When I left school I caught the 8.25 train every day to the city and worked in a newspaper office for three long years. Then one holiday when camping in a lakeland wood I felt really alive for the first time. I knew then that I had to go on living.

I got a job in the Lake District, as what the employment exchange called a 'forest worker', which about covered everything from cooking the staff meals to heavy navvying. I shall never know why my employer took me on; he must have seen me as a green towny who did not know one end of an axe from the other. He was not a man for compliments and the biggest one he ever paid me was when I was leaving to do my National Service. He shook me solemnly by my calloused hand and said, 'I shall miss your Shepherd's Pies.' Four and a half years in the Navy extinguished any remains of wanderlust, and I went back to the old urban charade. It was all very well living in the country, I told myself sternly, but what sort of a career could an ambitious young man make for himself there? Ambitious? The word nagged a little. The extent of my ambition was to have enough money to buy my freedom.

Then it came to me – as a sort of sickness. One morning I saw myself, not as myself, but like a character in a play. There I was: a man with a name which meant nothing. The face I saw reflected in the mirror was that of a stranger. The body I wore was not mine. I had lost my way.

For some days, I did not know what was wrong. Then I knew. I had to go back.

The Lake District to me was not the soft, mild, benevolent, romantic place that the holidaymaker knows; was not the wide, free fells or the challenging crags. It was all those, partly – and much, much more. It was, as I remembered, the smell of moist earth and newly cut wood; an aching back; rain in my face and wet feet; blisters on my hands; sore muscles; hard work, and a bitterness as well as deep and total satisfaction. The Lake District was my hard taskmaster, my teacher, my spiritual guide; never my mistress. I had to return.

I got off the bus at the old familiar stop and walked up the lane. I heard the bus grinding up the hill, taking the past and security with it, and leaving me squarely in the uncertain present. There was a cold east wind which shook the new lambs-tails catkins on the hazel hedge, and swirled the dry oak leaves at my feet.

The farm had not changed. With grey crags erupting out of its deep green fields it still looked as if it was wearing a thread-bare jacket, out at the elbows. The plough was propped in the same place, crazily against a crag outcrop. I remembered that during the War Emergency the farmer had been told by some-one in Whitehall to plough and sow corn on a certain per-centage of his acreage. The task nearly broke his back and his heart; and Charlie, his old horse, only survived it because of his sardonic sense of humour. The fields seem to grow stones here like some better grown potatoes; if you hit the ground with a pick it rings, and pretty well shatters your back teeth. I suppose moving glaciers after the Ice Age scooped away the soil like mother used to scrape off the surplus margarine from the bread in the bad lean days of the Depression. But the soil that is left is rich and allows good green grazing.

Beyond the farm and higher up the hill, the wood enclosed the lane. Bare oaks, some coppice with standards – a mixture of tall curving spindles and heavy pillars; lean rock crags poking through here and there with an odd yew tree and holly. Yews hereabouts are self-seeded and are common among the oaks. In local dialect, yews and oaks are 'yows and yaks'. Once when I asked the conductor of the country bus to put me off at the 'hill of oaks' stop he pretended not to understand. Then he affected inspiration: 'Do you mean "hill o' yaks" lad?'

There is a path, going left through the woods. It was once

pointed out to me that by standing at the path entrance, without moving you can count twenty-one varieties of trees. For here is a real mixture of hardwood and conifer including one huge spire of Norway spruce, and a massive beech. The path climbs between alders and sallows and birch and wild cherries, and sycamores and ashes; and there is an elder and a wych elm, sweet and horse chestnut, and larch, a crab and a group of tall Scots pines; an aspen, juniper, a poplar, several rowans and the ubiquitous 'yows and yaks'.

I took the path through the pines – there are red-squirrel dreys in their tops – and beyond on a tree-clothed rock terrace was the group of huts. A plume of smoke came from one chimney, and I walked to the hut below it and knocked on the door.

My employer shook me by the hand. He thanked me for my letter and he confirmed the arrangement we had reached, that he would be glad to have me on the understanding that he could only offer me my keep and a small wage, and I would be required to do the part-time job of general estate maintenance – drains, ditches and fences. He then took me to my living quarters – a wooden hut with a shingle roof and a large stone wood-burning fireplace. He explained that I would draw my water from a well in the back a hundred yards away.

I put my modest luggage on the bunk in the corner and leant my axe against the wall. There are two things you never leave

anywhere: your best girl and your axe. I thought of tea. I followed the beaten path to the well. There was a frog in it; but
that did not bother me. If the water was good enough for him I
would not object. The water was three feet deep and as clear as
crystal to its green slate bottom. That was the best cup of tea I
had tasted in years. I had arrived, I was truly home; I was content. All I had left to do before nightfall was make up and light
a fire and unpack.

2 The Hut

What I shall always remember most about the hut is the large wood-burning fireplace – and the smoke. The chimney was a traditional one for the Lake District: a straight, dry-stone cylinder tapering slightly inside as it went up. If you sat in the fireplace and looked up you could see a disc of sky and several iron hooks in silhouette. The structure was fine if you wanted to smoke hams or fish, or season walking-sticks; as an accessory to a heat producer it was a failure. If there was the slightest breeze from any direction the smoke would spread itself evenly between chimney and room in more or less equal proportions, which was why the once white walls had the appearance of very old ivory and the mounted fox heads, hunting trophies which hung on the walls, had a fine coating of brown dust, and their yellow eyes a slightly inebriated, glazed expression. The smell of the place reminded me of a kipper factory. I was soon thoroughly cured, inside and out!

At first the wood smoke brought distressing symptoms of choking and crying, and I was continually opening windows and doors – with little apparent effect except to sweep in cold draughts which swirled the smoke around. But after a week or so I was acclimatized, and I would laugh at the discomforts of half-asphyxiated visitors. Strangely, though, the symptoms returned to me every night when I retired to my bunk, which occupied a corner of the same room. I cried like a baby every time I tried to close my eyes. All my possessions began to smell of smoke; even my better clothes, which I kept in a closed cupboard under the bunk.

I soon became a connoisseur of wood smoke. For fragrance, in my opinion, there is little to match juniper; I would stack this wood aside against the days I had visitors. Apple and well-seasoned cherry are pure luxury too. Holly and birch have a clean tang. Ash, particularly green ash, smells like washing day. Old oak has an honest, pungent, lusty smell as you would expect. The other hardwoods are hardly worth a mention smokewise. The soft woods, pine, spruce or larch are rather vulgar; but there is something to be said for a really old vintage larch root.

Once one gets the taste for smoking wood it is possible to mix and obtain subtle flavours; and invent recipes. Prepare a fire base of larch kindling; add well-seasoned oak until the logs redden deeply; place one large back-log of holly, and add, from the fire back to the front, one crab-apple log, one of well-dried cherry and one of birch. An ideal after-dinner mixture.

I had very little in the way of furniture in my hut. One tired canvas-seated chair with a lumpy cushion occupied a corner of the rag hearth-rug, a varnished table and two oak forms stood in the middle of the room. To the right of the fireplace was the 'kitchen': a low cupboard with a metal top and two gas rings, fed from a cylinder, a cabinet with an assortment of crockery and cooking utensils, and a wash-bowl; the slops had to be emptied outside. To the left of the fireplace was a window, my bunk was in the corner, two windows and another bunk occupied the next wall. Opposite the fireplace the book shelves carried a variety of light reading – mainly thrillers and westerns. Next to these there was a rough wooden door into a store room. On the walls there were about a score of hunting trophies, of foxes and otters – sad, lifeless masks with perpetually hostile expressions. One, the head of a very old, large dog fox, probably had few teeth left when he was caught, for he was mounted with his mouth closed, and grinned as a consequence a very sinister grin. Below each stuffed head was a printed notice of the date and place of capture – all within fifteen miles or so. The dog fox was the only one caught in our wood. These staring, mostly vicious faces all around me, nature red in tooth if not in claw, added to the wilderness atmosphere of the place. They snarled at me as I arose each morning; drooled over my lonely meals; and dared me, at night, to put out my lights and retire.

The smoke; the trophies. But there was something else so often in the atmosphere of the hut, and it settled around me like an old cloak as I drank my tea. It was the utter and complete silence. On that first day the dry leaves lay undisturbed calf-deep about the doorway and the birds were too busy seeking food to utter a note between them. The silence was very real indeed and it made my heart pound.

As I drained my cup I was conscious of a tiny but persistent sound. I had left the door ajar and the sound came from outside. I could not put a name to it – a very faint lapping noise. I went outside to trace it. I had left the bucket of water which I had brought from the well under the fern-decked slate shelter made to house it, and the sound was coming from the bucket. A little shrew had fallen into the water and was swimming round and round the edge desperately, unable to scramble up the bucket side. I picked it out, and it lay shivering in my hand, a tiny warm spark of vital life. When it recovered sufficiently it made a move and I closed my hand to prevent the creature from dropping off. It rewarded me by sinking its little needle-like teeth into a finger, so I put it on to the bank. It raised its head – and its long nose curled upwards like a toy trunk, quivering in an effort to scent out its bearings. Several seconds passed and then it plunged under the matted grass and was gone.

The banks around the hut were well populated by shrews; both the common shrew and the pygmy – our smallest mammal, its head and body together being little more than two inches in length. Shrews are strange creatures, heard more often than seen if you have hearing which picks up their very high-pitched twitter. They are the most quarrelsome creatures, and the bad-tempered twittering usually accompanies fierce fights for territories and mates. Strangely, whenever they entered the hut in error, unlike voles and mice, they would get into a terrible panic on discovering the lack of natural cover and could not settle long enough to hide effectively. It was a simple matter to corner and pick them up, but they usually had good bites before I could release them outside. One of them I let go amused me by seizing a small earthworm, which lay across its getaway route, and shaking it in its temper, like a terrier with a rat. Shrews are worm and insect eaters with voracious appetites, and like moles, whose territories they often share, they die if they are without food for more than just a few hours. In the past such mysterious creatures were regarded with great superstition. It was thought that if one were to run over a child or a cow, they would be poisoned; the only remedy was to push an offending shrew into a hole made in an ash tree, then the tree would have special medicinal properties and could cure the mischief. Absurd, of course, yet the local farmer's wife, a down-to-earth woman if ever I knew one, was not at all happy when I told her about my shrew invasions.

Strangely, vole and mice holes were not evident in the woodwork of my room. Few country homes are free of these intruders unless a cat is kept, but I had no cat and it was some time before I discovered a possible explanation of the rodents' absence. I was returning from the well when I saw a small, snake-like, reddish creature emerge from the space along the bottom of the hut, and make a leisurely bounding course to a pile of stones on the bank. I was just getting over the first surprise when I saw another, and another, and two more, all following each other. A family of weasels, sleek-coated, beady-eyed and intent. I saw weasels several times after that over a long period. They were always about, and mice and voles and rats are their chief diet. Shrews on the other hand have an effective weapon against most predators – a nasty taste – and they are normally left alone. Thus my visitors.

The hut in which I had come to live was in a small railed enclosure. What had been the small kitchen garden was now a great bed of dry, blackened nettles. The bank above the rock shelf on which the hut stood was covered in large brown ferns and sparse turf and moss. The little yard on the south side was littered with the remains of a woodpile, and there was a still serviceable saw-horse and a knotty yew chopping-block. A grind-stone in the corner was rusted up and no longer responded to the handle. The yard and the paths were paved with dark slate, the old Silurian beds which are the foundations of the southern Lake District. One need not go far to find an outcrop to quarry into; that is why dry stone walls proliferate in the landscape of the area. They stride right up the fells, in many cases beyond the 2,000-foot contour. The amazing human giants

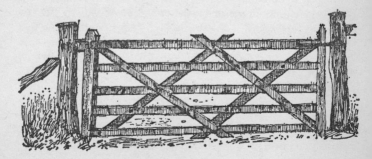

who engineered them a century ago and beyond, did not usually have to carry their material very far.

Oak trunks closely surrounded the enclosure and there was no view to speak of. Through a gap I could glimpse the fell which rose to the east, stark, broken with heather-strewn crags and dotted with juniper. A slate-flagged path curved away into the oaks towards the other huts; another at the other end snaked away into pines towards the well and to the great wood.

3   *The Great Wood*

The first time, as a boy, I plunged gaily and innocently into a
real forest, I might as well have been in a fiendishly conceived
labyrinth. It was a long time before I was convinced that I was
really lost. I think it happened when I found my own footprint
in a bog I was sure I had not come across before. One has to learn
the rules; the first one being to orientate oneself before one sets
out. My hut was on the eastern side of the wood. The cold wind
came from the north east. The land rose to the north, right the
way from east to west. A fitful sun made its presence occasion-

ally known in the south west. One learns to check these things constantly, as well as the way one has already walked.

In a hardwood or mixed forest it is easy to see that every tree has its own recognizable and unique character. Some of them are unusually shaped – a branch coming out at a strange angle on a Douglas fir, an acute twist in a larch bole, a stag-headed oak tree, a birch with semi-weeping branches, an ash trunk scraped by deer antlers, a beech with an unusually knotted root; as well as the more obvious ones: headless from a lightning strike; or with an unusually grotesque shape; or birches with heavy growths of 'witch's brooms' – masses of tightly-packed twigs caused by fungus attacks.

Each living tree is in effect a colony of plants. Each single leaf in the crown has its stem reaching down the twig, and the branch, and the trunk, to the root. Each is a plant, clasped tightly with its brethren around the dead core of its mass of forebears.

In the embryo, in his mother's womb, the shape and form of a man is already made. The ripe seed of a tree is by comparison only a mere suggestion, a general proposition, the soul rather than the image. Once the shoot and roots burst outwards the plant is subject only to the general law which governs its species, and its remaining existence is what its own immediate environment and climate make of it. It must fight for its own share of light and nourishment; every twist and turn and bulge of the trunk, every buttress on its bole, is a gesture of aggression or defence. Each tree is an army of plants, grouped around the dead inherited spine, and fighting for life. A tree is a battle hymn. If you put your ear to its trunk on a windy day you can hear it.

The trail from the hut into the great wood, as I came to think of it, forked beyond the pines, and in my first exploration on the day of my arrival I took the steeper track to the west so that I could follow and view the setting sun from some high point. I had not gone far before I found the first pitstead. A pitstead is a small, man-made terrace cut into the hillside and is a common sight in the hillside forests of the southern Lake District. When the new industrial iron age exploded into our civilization, charcoal was in great demand. Iron ore was pulled out of the depths of the Lake District's mines, and charcoal was taken from its wooded hills. The making of charcoal was an exacting art. It demanded a flat base to work on, and a very slow burning wood fire, stacked and turfed with great care with air admitted at precise places in measured amounts. The charcoal burner tended his fires day and night, living in a rough hut of his own making, close by. He would be cutting the wood, digging his pitsteads, and burning, all at the same time – a tough and hardy giant among men.

Oaks predominated on the slopes. Most of it was coppice of great age. But there were groups of other species. If one fails to recognize the individual trees the groups are easier to pick out, for tree families group themselves in woods as human families and ethnic races do in cities. And as human groups often pool and share their resources, so do the trees. They will even share their root systems; each one grafting itself, merging itself into its neighbour's, passing on and sharing nourishment. So one sees groups of alders crowding into the wet places; birch thickets around the rocks; the larch grove on the steep slope; the groups of hazel filling in the gaps. A mixed woodland can be a place of sustaining beauty to behold.

The trail was rough and rocky. By comparison with the spikey crag lines of the hills of the central areas of the Lake District, the southern fells have a softer shape. But there was nothing soft about the ground. The great wood was in fact a huge slate crag; the beds had been tipped almost vertically, sloping upwards from east to west. The glaciers of the ice age had carved away the western side to leave a steep slope, a summit of bare, sharp crags and a rough western face dropping to the lake. The whole scene was broken up into pockets and great ledges and miniature valleys; it had no doubt been forest since the Ice Age – mainly oak, alder, birch, and hazel. It must have been a sparse covering at first, until the weather and the trees themselves got about the business of soil-making.

My track levelled off after a while on to a ledge. There was a clearing of grass, still whitened by the morning's frost, and beyond that in soft wet ground were deer prints – the sharp little 'slots' left by a family of roe deer; and one large print left by a wandering red-deer stag. This was an exciting find. I hoped I might see some deer.

Then my way vanished into a swamp and I skirted round it to the north to see if I could pick the track up on the other side. This detour brought me to an enormous rock slab, pitched at a forty degree angle and about a hundred feet high. Half hidden behind oaks and pines it looked smooth and scarcely climbable, until a closer look through a gap as I approached revealed cracks and fissures, green with heather and juniper. It was a miniature replica of the Great Slab of Bowfell, several miles west. One of the remarkable things about the Lake District is the way a scenic theme repeats itself time and time again, with decorative variations.

I climbed it by a 'rake' – a diagonal groove running from the middle of the base to an upper corner. On the top of this crag there was plateau to the west, and the trees here, mainly larch and old oaks, had been twisted into grotesque shapes by the winds. By this time it was about an hour from sunset. The western sky was red and streaked with high, brilliantly phosphorescent cloud. To the north-west was a hog-back of rock skirted with burnished dead bracken. I noticed something move there . . . and my heart leaped as a huge figure rose steadily from the bracken and moved towards the rock crest. It was a red stag. Caught in the rays of the sun its coat glowed like fire, its great antlers gleamed like red-hot metal. It lifted its head high and stood motionless, as its nostrils sniffed in search of confirmation of what its erect ears had warned. It was staring directly at me and I stood still, scarcely able to breath, as it waited in a sort of furious disdain for either movement or scent from me. It was one of those moments when time slips into another dimension. There was an utter silence and nothing moved in the scene at all; It was as if the whole mechanism of time and living had jammed. I cannot remember how long we stood thus. Although red deer were not uncommon in this area, and although this one was of magnificent but no exceptional size, the sight of that first-day burning stag with the red-hot antlers etched itself as deeply as anything into my memory.

A flurry of light wind decided the issue as it bent the dead bracken stalks and carried a message to the stag. I saw the animal start as if electrocuted – the front legs lifted, then stiffened in a brief gesture of majestic ill-temper, and with one leap he was gone from me beyond the skyline.

But I had not seen all. I made for the hog-back where I had last seen the deer, with my heart singing, through the dead bracken and the blasted larches, towards the red sun. I climbed the rock only to see another, sharper crest of rock beyond framed in blood-red, beheaded trees like butchered sacrifices round a fire-lit altar. I crossed to it and climbed, and the unexpected view came as a joyous shock. Below me the great wood tumbled steeply over the broken ground, with crag upon crag thrusting through the rolling breakers of the tree tops. At the foot, like burnished copper, the water – the shining levels of the long lake.

My eyes lingered there, then up the far afforested shore with its now sharp shadows, and beyond to the rolling fells. Then, for a finale at the end of some monumental symphony – the mountain peaks; from Dow and the Old Man of Coniston, through the Crinkles, Bowfell, Great End, the Pikes of Langdale and High White Stones – the summit snows glowing here, but there blue-shadowed; and to the north Fairfield horseshoe, Dollywagon, and the blue haze of the high fells of Cumberland.

I stood there for perhaps half an hour before I started back. And I suppose if there is any logic in the order in which destiny arranges the succession of human experiences, it should all have been left at that. Nothing more of any lasting significance should have been allowed to happen that day. It was as if I had been, by a divine choice, privileged to approach the golden gates of paradise. It left me breathless, elated and awed. I should have been allowed to return to my hut, without any distraction, to meditate, on clouds of woodsmoke. But it was not to be.

I picked up the track I had lost on my way up and this time, on reaching the swamp, struck off down-hill to my right, and below it. The swamp emptied itself into a cheerful little beck, and I stopped to admire the way it spilled itself down a rock step, green-velveted with moss. And as I stood there I had a sudden feeling that I was being observed. I looked up to the erect figure of a man, grey-haired and bearded, leaning with one hand on a large chestnut tree at the other side of the beck. He wore a short, faded yellow gaberdeen raincoat, tied round the waist with baler twine, blue dungaree trousers, and wellington boots cut off short below the calf. His eyes had a strange wild expression and he seemed to be some sort of tramp.

'I saw you – ' he said, very slowly with a slightly, hoarse voice. 'I saw you – move in.' There was a long silence, while I stood struck dumb with surprise. He nodded his head over his shoulder.

'I'm your neighbour. Live over there.'

'Oh?' I said. There was another long pause.

'Perfect weather?' I ventured nervously.

He nodded. His eyes glowed and he thrust his head forward as if he was going to whisper some vital secret.

'Did you see – ' he asked, ' – him?' I had no notion what he was talking about, and said nothing.

'Michael?' he asked.

'Michael?' I asked.

'Michael!' he exclaimed loudly, his eyes wilder than ever. 'Michael and all his angels fighting the great dragon!'

I could feel my skin prickling with goose pimples. There was another seemingly endless silence. I searched for some means of escape, my fuddled thoughts struggling for some hint of sane explanation. I was beginning to think, without much confidence, that he was referring in some allegorical way to the splendid sunset when he suddenly cried out:

'Did you see the four beasts with six wings?'

'Well – no,' I said feebly after another terrible pause.

The wildness then seemed to go out of his eyes, and he turned as if about to go. I stepped over the steam ready to take off from his route at a suitable tangent. Then he suddenly wheeled about.

'Beware!' he cried.

My hair practically stood on end.

'Beware of the archangel Gabriel! Traitor! And the angel of the bottomless bottomless pit!'

Suddenly he turned and was gone, walking with great strides through the oaks.

I picked up my track again and made down for the hut, my thoughts in terrible confusion. It was cold in the hut clearing and in deep shade. I picked up an armful of logs, went indoors, and was about to bolt the door in an attempt to shut out any further confusion of impressions until I could collect myself, when I heard footsteps.

Luckily it was not the neighbour in the old raincoat but my employer.

'Just passing on my way home,' he said. 'Settled in all right?'

I told him that I indeed had, but mentioned my encounter. He laughed.

'You saw old Natty then! Don't mind him. Daft as an old gosling! He's harmless. Tragedy really. A well educated chap. Sometimes comes in the wood for edible fungus. Not poisoned himself yet, so he can't be all that daft. I suppose he went on about his friend the archangel Gabriel? He usually gets around to him. Poor old Natty. Never mind. Good night!'

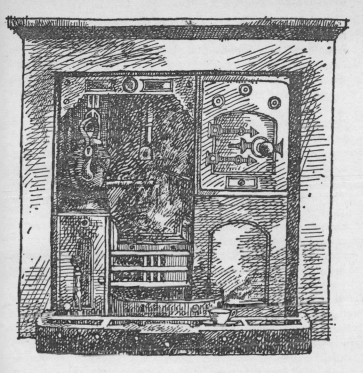

4　Chores; and Neighbours

I never imagined that life would always be easy at my new home. The exhilaration, such as I had experienced on my first day there, would come, I expected, as compensation between bouts of discomfort and drudgery. The accommodation was spartan and there were no modern conveniences; bottled gas was the only recent installation. Water had to be carried, and all the fuel cut, carried, sawn and split. The lavatory was in a tin shack, and its bucket had to be emptied once a week in a pit dug for the purpose in hard, rocky, rooty earth. Washing was done on a shelf in a back porch, open to cutting east winds; and in the same spot I endured stand-up baths which were accomplished very rapidly indeed, and as much, I felt, for the cleansing of the soul as the body. Milk and eggs were collected from the farm a mile down the hill as the nearest shop was in the village five miles away. I had no radio, and the newspapers which were passed on to me were days old. Solitude I could bear because I had books, a trunkful of which I had sent on in advance; and I had my typewriter and a back-log of work.

I organized my days carefully. Monday was washing day, weather permitting. Friday was cleaning day, and Saturday was for shopping. Sunday was for recreation. At that time although I had a belief of sorts, I had no time for religious services; and anyway I guessed that if I attempted the tortuous journey over the fell roads to the nearest church on my old bicycle most of my praying would be done before I got there.

My daily routine began with woodcutting for fuel. There is, of course, a mystique about wood burning. Some have romantic visions of crouched and muffled figures dragging log-laden sledges through a savage landscape of snow and ice; frost-bearded Vikings with massive axes, round great fires of pine logs; or raw-boned Northerners squatting over faggot-heated porridge pots. Many town dwellers burn wood for pleasure. One man I know did very well once out of selling 'yule logs' by post. His romantic northern-sounding address, evocative of resinous forest smells and ice-wracked lakes, helped his business more than a little. His customers were not buying fuel but the magic of dreams and memories of childhood story books.

All wood-burning pundits have their prejudices and the commonest one is against elm. It will not burn, they say; or it 'burns cold'. Only wych elm grew in the wood, and it burned for me quite well when dry. For common elm I cannot speak, but the age-old superstition that elm 'loveth not mankind' persists. Does it not, without warning, drop its boughs? It does. And is it not the best wood for coffins? It is. Yet I knew a Wiltshire man who said that he burned hardly anything else; and it was very fine, he said, when well seasoned.

Ash is the darling of the wood burners. It cuts well, and splits beautifully, and burns even when it is green; and it is a fast grower. Alder burns well, dry; but if you use it exclusively you will be sawing all day. Sycamore and birch, too, burn fast; so for long-lasting stuff you need oak, beech and, best of all, hawthorn: all splendid when well seasoned. But holly logs are in a class of their own. Yew, too – but this wood is like iron and will break or blunt your axe, your saw, and your spirit. Of the soft woods pine is good, and larch as well if you are in a hurry for a blaze and prepared to roll back the hearth-rug in preparation for the spectacular fusillade.

Wood burning is so aesthetically pleasing. Every log, as it is picked up, can be examined as an individual work of art – shape, grain, colour, weight – before being placed carefully on the fire in the correct position, to give its own artistic display of pyrotechnics. And in an idle moment by the fire's warmth you can take a knife and improve on the art of nature, carving into the wood, or cutting designs into the bark. Or you can play building and balancing games.

I had to gather kindling too, for storing in a dry place. Larch and pine logs could be split small and dried by the fire; or kindling could be gathered 'raw'. Holly again would be my first choice. The thin dead twigs from a holly tree will start a fire even if gathered wet and then merely shaken. But hollies are rather miserly with their dead twigs, and the only worthy substitute, with a generous yield, is birch. I have won several bets in my time from workmates, by starting a fire outdoors, in heavy rain, without the use of any dry medium such as paper. The trick is easy if there are birch trees about; then there is always an abundance of dead twigs which can be snapped easily off the trunks. From these can be gathered a handful of needle-thin stuff that can be pushed into a pocket while you collect slightly thicker material. A good pile is made of the birch twigs; then, when all is ready, the handful of needle-thins is taken from the pocket (where they have left much of their moisture), put into the fire centre, and carefully lit with a match. The wood contains sufficient natural oil to start the fire well.

Once kindled, stoking the fire can be a work of art. A large back-log is necessary; it should be heavy hardwood – fresh-cut green stuff will do at a pinch – and this acts as a reflector. Holly is the best, and a good log will burn for two days; a really good green one will last for several days. The morning fire should be re-kindled from the back-log of the previous day: a smart blow with the poker to break off its embers, small kindling on top of these, a puff with the bellows or breath and she is away.

In winter, fuel was my first chore. Cooking was another necessary routine. I soon learned to be miserly with the gas, for the heavy steel cylinders had to be lugged up from the entrance gate on my back. There was an iron kettle which could be slung over the fire. I preferred therefore to use one of the iron hooks in the chimney, and stews could be made on the fire if the pan was stood on the iron pan stand close by. An occasional roast was possible if I noosed the meat in a rabbit snare and hung it on the roasting hook at the chimney front. But this meant turning and basting – demanding constant attention; and if one is really hungry after a day outdoors – watching a sizzling, fragrant morsel turning before one's eyes is a long agony of mouth-watering suspense. Far better to clap the meat in a closed pot with onions and carrots and think of other things for an hour.

I have never found cooking an unpleasant task. I had some cookery books to help out: one was a battered gem which included wild foods and flavourings with its ingredients. A stew for instance, with jack-by-the-hedge (or garlic-mustard) leaves to give a subtle country flavour. Tansy pudding: made with breadcrumbs, milk and eggs, and chopped tansy leaves. And a traditional dish of the Lake District: 'Easter ledgers', a tasty physic for the countrymen of the pre-can and freezer days, who lived on a winter diet of salt pork, bacon and cereals. This was made from any of the first spring greens such as cabbage leaves, cauliflower or broccoli sprigs, or brussel sprouts tops; and to these were added first and foremost the fresh green leaves of ledgers (bistort), which gave the fine subtle flavour; young nettle leaves, watercress; gooseberry and raspberry leaves new burst; mint, sour docks, jack-by-the-hedge, and a few dandelion leaves. These should be washed and chopped finely, a handful of barley added; and the whole tied into a cloth to simmer in a pan until the liquid is nearly gone. Turn out, add a knob of butter, salt and pepper, and you have a rich dish to make you fighting fit!

Every day I walked down to the farm for milk. The walk was a pleasant one and very often it brought the day's only human contact. Tom, the farmer, was only too willing to knock off work for a few minutes to talk about the weather, or his ewes and lambing prospects. He was proud of his stock but not a man for superlatives.

'What do you think of that then?' pointing to his best tup; a sturdy, restless, superior and scornful looking creature, indignant at being penned.

I would express admiration.

'Aye,' he would say, 'It'll do.'

Everything that was fine, and strong, and growing like mad, and profitable would 'do'.

Mrs C. was a shy, kind, motherly individual who was interested to know how I could possibly get on without a woman's help. Men, to her, were useless, ham-fisted, untidy and clumsy animals indoors, and she was sure for most of the time that I was starving, not keeping myself decently 'wrapped up', and living in conditions of squalor. She would not, of course, visit me to see for herself. But she invited me into the farm kitchen if she had the chance, and pressed pint-pots of strong tea on to me, and great slabs of currant pasty or ginger-bread. Tom would ask me if I could 'give him a hand' sometimes. This, I eventually suspected, could well have been an excuse to give me a huge meal in payment. After forcing down a plateful of roast meat and vegetables, followed by a substantial pudding, the final assault on my finely timed digestive system would be by cheese and biscuits. 'Cheese?' Thud! Half a pound of best

Lancashire on my plate with a handful of biscuits; then the walk back to the hut with a stomach stretched tight against my loosened belt.

Joe, the farm hand, an agile lad of seventy or thereabouts, was a beaming friendly man without any conversation at all; but he was willing to offer what he had when we met. 'Why, aye' would be the answer to any opening remark.

'Good weather, Joe!'

'Why, aye!'

'Are you feeling well, Joe?'

'Why, aye!'

'Days are lengthening nicely again.'

'Why, aye!'

There were cheery 'Why, ayes', and wise 'Why, ayes' (given with a knowing nod); and sad 'Why, ayes' (with a slow shake of the head).

It was a pleasure to watch Joe 'lig' a hedge; for the work was his pride and joy. Hedges around where we were are a wild mixture of hawthorn, hazel, ash and holly. Laying a hedge is necessary when it grows too tall and shows gaps. Bough undergrowth is cut away, leaving the bared upright stems which are then cut only part-way through near the butt, then pulled over and layed in neat lines, occasionally being pinned firm with hazel stakes. The tools for the job are a pair of leather hedging mitts, one very sharp bill-hook, and a stone to whet it with at regular intervals. Joe made it all look so simple.

My attempts at the few yards here and there of woodland boundary hedges were, by comparison, pitiful. Getting the bill-hook really sharp and cutting away the undergrowth and unwanted wood was one thing. But striking the stems in the right place with just the right amount of cut was another. If the cut was too light the stem could not be bent over without breaking; and it was almost impossible to correct my error with another cut in exactly the same spot. Too hard a blow could take the hook right through the stem, which was worse. Joe once watched me attempting the work and never said a word; not even a 'Why, aye', but I could tell he was suffering. Next time I went along to finish the section it was done. Joe had done it on his day off. All he would accept in recompense was a bundle of bean sticks.

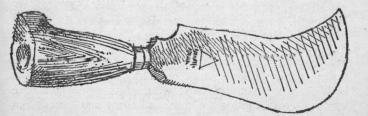

5   *The Coppice*

I had arrived as winter was having its last fierce fling. Contrary to what most people might think, the valleys of the Lake District normally have a mild winter with little snow – far less, for instance, than the south east of England. The prevailing west wind from the sea brings that warmer, moist air which makes for good green grass and, where the soil is deep enough, tall trees. The exposed Shap Fell on the eastern edge of the Lake District suffers from snow storms, but this is outside the Lake District proper. A bit of north in the wind can bring snow to the mountain tops, with a good chance that it might linger long. But on the whole the valleys and villages have a comfortable time of it. Strangely, hardly anyone believes this. The Lake District is *North*. It borders on Scotland, which every Sassenach knows is snow- and ice-locked from November to March. Not many of us remember that Britain is in the same latitudes as Moscow and Quebec, and it is only the warm currents of the Atlantic washing our western shores that keep our climate mild. And so there is a greater difference in climate between the west and east of our islands, than between the south and north. But ideas die hard. Even now my good friends, who ought to know better, arrive for visits in winter with their cars loaded with coats, blankets, flasks and shovels. More often than not they arrive to a mild sunny day and we all have a good laugh about it.

A good long frost is not all that common, and a good long lake freeze happens only once or twice in a lifetime. Skaters have to seek out the shallower small lakes and tarns. Skiers seek out the north-east-facing fells. But the last fling of that first winter brought snows and cold weather, and my first job of coppice thinning.

No work could be better on a cold morning. There is the walk to the job through a white and silent wood. A silence that one can actually *feel*. Not just an absence of noise; but an experience. Snow brings a splendid opportunity to check the animal tracks. I was surprised to see the large number of roe deer signs. Family parties were moving about the woods in numbers. By comparison with the large red deer stags and hinds, the roe bucks and does are small and light – no larger than a greyhound. They are beautiful creatures, perfectly designed for their woodland environment: slim, long-legged, highly agile, and very fast. They have a strange, fairy-like quality which puts them in a class entirely of their own. There is something which seems so utterly British about a splendid red deer stag. It is so strong, brave, silent, stiff-upper-lippish and defiantly enduring. But the shy, ghost-like roe, timid and swift, belong surely to the Robin Hood period in our history. In fact its history goes way back beyond that by many thousands of years. Roe were here long before the Ice Age and long before the first human settlers. Their British pedigree is probably not matched by any other mammal. They have been native to the woods of northern England, and to Scotland and Wales, since pre-history; and have survived the many alien pressures on what we call the 'balance of nature' because of their remarkable hardiness, mobility and secrecy.

I know a forest worker who said that in seven years working in one particular wood where roe were plentiful he had never seen one. He had seen their tracks, and he had certainly seen the damage that the bucks had done; for their habit of 'fraying' young saplings, scraping away the bark with their antlers to mark their territory at rutting time, makes them a great nuisance to forestry. But he had never seen a roe deer. He may have been very slow, and a bit short sighted; and he was no doubt a noisy character; but credit to the alert and silent roe.

It was on coppice thinning that I first met Dave. The oak coppice was in the north east corner of the wood and I had arranged to meet my workmate by a pool in the beck that flowed through it. First news of Dave's coming was announced by a jay – its grating cry rang out as his great feet thudded over a wall gap; then muffled sounds of movement increased in volume until his progress was heralded by breaking twigs and crackling bracken – and loud cursing as he caught his face, head and elbows on obstructions. Then at last the thicket parted to reveal his red, cheerful face. He broke through the bracken, stumbled into the clearing, and said, 'Doctor Livingstone, I presume!'

His great red hand took hold of my still soft one and shook it like a dog shaking a rat. 'I'm Dave,' he said, 'You're pale and your hands want roughening up. We'll take care of that, eh?'

He threw down his 'bait bag' – the old gas-mask haversack that contained his lunch – then picked it up again to shake his vacuum flask to see if it was still intact. I discovered later that Dave surely had the world record for flask breaking.

'Well, lad,' he said, 'Here are the union rules. Tea break at ten. Bait at twelve-thirty. Knock off at five, and no extra time for injuries. Nice, steady pace. If it rains – we get wet.'

He took off his jacket and hung it on an oak branch, putting his foot on his haversack in the process, and cursing. He then rolled up the sleeves of his screaming-red sweater and started work.

'Well, my little yaks. Let's be having you, then.'

His first cut – clean and smooth with just the right amount of swinging effort, no more and no less – convinced me of his skill. Soon wood chips as large as bread slices were flying, and his first stem fell.

I joined him, and my numbed fingers soon began to burn. We accumulated a stack – and a problem. It is one thing to fell timber, quite another to clean up as one goes along. Though Dave was a smooth worker with an axe, he was a clumsy oaf when it came to clearing and stacking branches. He somehow, in the course of that morning, and on every day subsequently, managed to entangle himself, his axe, his sweater and his boots, at every opportunity, and his language and his bursts of temper were really choice. He blundered about with his burden of branches like some legendary giant at grips with a many-tentacled monster; teeth gritted and a ghastly look of aggressive rage on his red face, which reminded me of the aspect recommended to his troops by Henry the Fifth at Harfleur. Occasionally he would let out a scream: 'Hell take you, you ...' If the thing he was battling with was really formidable enough to make him lose control, anything could happen. Green oak branches as thick as my wrist would be snapped like match-wood, and I downed tools and watched with admiration.

When we had collected a good pile of branches we fired it and began to get some elbow room; but it did not lessen Dave's predicament. There was now the added fire hazard; and his wretched burdens, which he threw on the blaze, would grab him at the last moment and attempt to drag him in, too. Eyebrows, the front of his hair, and all the hair on his arms, were soon consumed by the great heat; which was ably matched in intensity by his language.

But Dave also offered more entertainment. He carried a haunted carborundum stone. Every time he sought it to put an edge on his axe it had vanished. He would feel around in the snow and wood chippings, muttering a variety of impatient expletives until his patience ended and his voice, almost falsetto with rage, screeched. 'Hell take the thing!' He would eventually discover it under his boot, or on a tree stump where he had put it so as to find it easily; or in his back pocket. And then he took it all out on the axe edge.

We worked steadily forward through the oaks doing a job which must give work to every muscle in the body, for you are swinging, cutting, bending, and turning, and stretching, pulling and pushing all the time. Dave was a good worker. He appeared to be unhurried but he was getting through twice as much work as I was, even with his wrestling matches to interrupt the flow. There was new daylight where we had worked; straight single stems instead of the jungle of lesser ones from the same stools. Neat stacks of wood and the fire, a great mad hungry thing, crackling and hissing noisily at its meal.

We were tackling some particularly crooked and awkward oak shoots when I noticed Dave suddenly drop his axe as if his fingers had become paralysed. I took another swing.

'Stop!' he called, 'Are you mad?'

I looked at him as he stared at me with wide-eyed horror. I suppose I stared back with incomprehension.

'It's twelve-thirty,' he said slowly. 'Bait time. Drop that axe at once!'

I comprehended; then caught my lunch bag that he threw at me. We sat on logs and we fell to with no more ceremony, I to my bacon sandwiches, Dave to his thick bread slices, rich yellow cheese, and an aggressive raw onion.

Lunch was spiced with the rich smell of new-cut oak – rich and sweet like old cider. And inevitably, a robin pecking about the new boot-churned earth and snow, with one eye watching us. He took the morsels I threw away to eat. Was it the same bird that returned time after time? No single bird could put all that away.

Over the tea flasks, Dave talked. About his brother in Australia who had done well for himself; and another brother in the army; and another in London; and another who was stockman on a big Yorkshire farm; and another who went in for pigs in a big way in Cheshire; and – I asked him how many brothers he had.

'Ten,' he said. 'We had a football team of our own, we had. I'm youngest. Got one sister. Father said she was a mistake. But she's a good un. Best cook in t'county. Tough as they come, but a heart of gold.'

He threw a lump of fruit cake at me.

'Try that for size, and see what I mean.'

It must have been 98 per cent fruit. Moist, substantial.

'I see what you mean,' I said.

Stoking the fire in the lunch hour was apparently not against union rules; and the blue smoke rose straight in the frosty air. I asked Dave how far the oak coppice went, and he told me that northwards it thinned out into an alder swamp ('allers' to Dave), with a birch jungle in the middle, with a few old yows and big old spruce split right down the middle with a thunderbolt. I resolved to look at it. Then westwards, he said, the coppice thinned out into some 'right bonny' spruces.

'Come on,' he said, 'I'll show you something for your money.'

He led me through, and sometimes under, the coppice as the ground rose. Then we came to a drainage ditch and into some fine firs. Straight and broad.

'Nay,' he said, as I admired them, 'Come on.'

The air was still among the spruces. The light dimmed and took on a special quality. I felt that I was among the great columns of a cathedral. The ground was thick with a needle carpet and had only thin patches of snow, and we made absolutely no sound as we walked. Not even a bird stirred. As we went in deeper the sunlight streamed in golden shafts here and there between the varied shades of green. And light that was filtered trickled down; pure, softened and restrained; like light from stained-glass windows.

Dave beckoned as the ground began to rise. Then there it was – an amazing sight.

'We call this Galleon's glade,' said Dave. At once I saw why.

A long time ago (eighteen ninety-odd, Dave said), a stand of nicely matured spruces were struck by a violent storm which skittled them all to the ground. Part of their roots were still in good earth so they continued to live on. But all plants grow upwards to the light, and the growing tips curved upwards like the prows of ships. And the side branches, which were now uppermost, grew up straight like ships' masts, each developing branches and foliage like rigging and sails; specially realistic sails as they were now, white with snow. To see one, growing in this way to a unique maturity, would be a sight indeed. But to see a whole squadron of them – twenty or thirty, all on the same course, on a brown sea spattered with snow foam, and frozen in utter silence, was a fantastic experience.

After we had feasted our eyes enough, Dave said, 'Come on,' and we returned to our work.

Dave had lost his carborundum; and after some strong language he stood on it. It was under his 'bait bag'.

6 *The Desert Island*

I had resolved to visit the 'island' in the 'aller' swamp, mentioned by Dave, with its blasted spruce. The next break in the coppice thinning made this possible.

We immediately started up two roe deer on the fringes of the swamp – an old doe and a young buck, probably mother and son. They wore their winter coats of grey, their rumps were pure white. They made off in a leisurely fashion for roe, stopping and turning once, as we froze still, to wrinkle their large black muffles in search of our scent, and turning their large ears in our direction.

The next discovery was red deer slot – deep tracks in the melting snow. These were fresh, and Dave picked up some droppings to see if they were still warm.

'Cold. Must have winded us long ago. A big stag by the looks of it. This is a great area for deer.'

The oak gave way to hazels and Dave pointed out the tracks of red squirrel: 'Scrambling around for his stores.'

Red squirrels (there are no grey in the Lake District) do not fully hibernate and can often be seen in winter. I made a mental note to buy monkey nuts to entice them to the hut.

We were soon up to our ankles in the swamp. The alders and birch were thick, tall, and spindly. The stems were racing and fighting upward for the light. The losers in the fight lay all rotten about us, like the broken pillars of Pompeii. Others, only just losing the race, rotted as they stood, crumpling at a touch and showering us with fragments. Dying birches had their characteristic brown and white fungi, *Piptoporus betulinus*, clasped round the stems like large kidney-bowls. As tough as old boot leather, I was once told that they served as razor strops for countrymen of old, and a dye was extracted from them.

We walked through this jungle of tree stems to a deep drain of clear running water.

'Look at that,' Dave said. 'Cut a hundred years ago I'll bet, that old drain, and as good as new. A great place for otters.'

We crossed it with a jump. Dave caught the sleeve of his sweater on a tree snag and cursed roundly, and then we were ascending a dry island of oaks and yews.

There was something about this place that appealed to me. It is difficult to explain why. It was an attractive piece of old woodland surrounded by a thick jungle, and with a man-made moat on two sides and a trout stream curving round the rest. This stream was called Stybeck, and it fed a tarn before descending to the large lake. This was obviously an enchanted island, behind and beyond the dark woods.

The lightning-shattered spruce was a spectacle. Its top had

gone, and lay, partly lodged, in an oak. From its broken jagged trunk-top to the root was a long spiralling split. The turf and soil about the large surface roots had been blasted away into crooked furrows. I was glad that I had not been around when the massive blow had struck.

There are some times and places where one has the strong impression that one has stood there in identical circumstances. At some time in the past the present moment had been dreamed of in detail, and one experiences a strange leap of the heart, and a breathless waiting for the next event which you know will come. The normal concept of time is shattered. This has been predicted.

This was one of the circumstances. I had stood and looked at that spruce before. This frozen violence. But more, that shattered remnant had a great message of almost cosmic significance; and I seemed to be upon the brink of understanding it. The tall broken finger pointing to the blue sky; the sweeping curve of the long split; the smashed earth about the roots – they had some meaning that just evaded me. I was poised on the threshold of knowing. This spell was broken by the half-expected movement which caught the corner of my eye. The brown leaves of a wintering fern were lifting and falling with a slight unfelt breeze. The plant appeared to be breathing in its sleep, silently and regularly. And the trees around stood, and watched, and waited as if I was the next actor in a drama, and had been given my cue.

'Come on lad!' Dave called and I followed him reluctantly to the far end of the island through another swamp to a point where the trout stream poured through a culvert in a boundary wall. And there below us down a rock slope, beyond the fringe of the wood, was a quiet little lake – a tarn. Another shining level that was mirror still, reflecting the hills beyond perfectly, except at the edges where the image was blurred by ice.

I carried back to my hut the memory of that island encounter in the swamp. And I reflected, over my evening's cooking, about the significance of its minor revelation, without a conclusion. A wind had got up by the time I had reached coffee and book stage. The trees about the hut swayed with each gust, and there was a noise in their tops like sea breakers; wave on wave. The door rattled and smoke poured in on me worse than ever. I was startled then when I heard a knock on the door.

It was the Major – my employer. He had part of a haunch of venison he wished to dispose of and thought I might like it. He had shot a poor specimen of a stag the day previously. He explained over a coffee that he had been after the beast for some time. It had a 'bad head' and he did not like the idea of its breeding and perpetuating its malformity. He had shot it from North Crag – a good vantage point, he assured me, as the deer fed below on a small plateau, and scent, if conditions were right, was lost.

He was clearly pleased with his shot and accepted another coffee as he expanded on the art of deer stalking.

'Walk on your heels. That's the secret. And watch your step for dry sticks. Don't be in a hurry, and don't put your full weight on your foot until you're sure it won't be noisy. God your chimney smokes!'

He reminded me to be sure to slit the meat and put bacon into the slits as it cooked. Venison, he explained, was a dry meat.

I would have enjoyed his company longer, but he clearly wanted to escape the smoke. I invited him to dinner on the Saturday evening coming and was glad when he accepted.

'Try cleaning the chimney,' he said, as he retreated into the night.

Dave told me how to clean the chimney, in the coppice on the following day.

'Get a lump of holly bush,' he said. 'Tie it on a weighted line. Get on the roof, drop down the weight; then get indoors and haul the holly down.'

It sounded easy.

'But don't get too big a holly lump, like Sam Dixon did, him over the fell. He got stuck damned hard. And firing the chimney didn't help. It was a right picnic. We had to damn near pull the house down to get it out. It took four of us, and half a barrel of ale. And I fell off the ladder too.'

'Were you hurt?'

'Well, no. Luckily I had a soft landing.'

'Soft landing?'

'Well,' said Dave with a sickly smile, 'Right in his muck heap. It was warm, too, I can tell you!'

To make sure I had got it right Dave cut the piece of holly himself. 'Porcupine holly', he called it. I had never noticed until then that holly varied so much in shape and prickliness. These leaves were extra curly and pointed. 'Right scratchity,' Dave said.

When I got back I tied a line to it and tied a metal bar at the other end. No ladder was needed to get on to the low-hanging roof. I dropped the weight down the chimney and went indoors and pulled. The holly scratched its way downwards and did the trick only too well. It took quite a time to clean up. But on lighting the fire again I found that it smoked almost as badly. Straight up flues are obviously not a success. I have never understood why.

I baked the venison in a biscuit-tin oven which I sat on the gas ring. It was a success, though I had no red-currant jelly to serve with it.

For the Saturday evening I got a piece of local home-cured bacon, and baked it in the same way as the venison; and I boiled some butter beans. My employer arrived promptly at seven, and we enjoyed the meal with creamed potatoes.

I had banked up a good fire – for a hot fire smokes less – and afterwards we drew up our chairs and helped ourselves from a jug of coffee standing at the hob. My employer lit up a cigar and talked where he had left off – about deer stalking.

There are many ways of attaining the various levels of human bliss. But one of the highest states of mental, spiritual and physical happiness is readily reached by way of a good meal, pleasant company, and easy seats by a good log fire. (Preferably there should be a vague impression of cold weather in the night outside your cosy room.) The cares of the world are lost. There is a magical presence. You feel a love for all humanity. Every remark made by your friend is a precious pearl of wisdom, and everything you say, encouraged by the warm smiles of your companion, is the essence of all your years of struggle and experience. You can suddenly recall incidents of the past, vividly, and they take on a meaning which they never had before.

The Major responded to the atmosphere eventually. First diffidently, he began to tell me about his younger days. He had run off to sea. Had worked at various jobs in the United States, served in the army, and eventually took to lumberjacking in Canada. And when he warmed to his subject he told me that on occasions he had 'taken off' into the wilderness with little more than a gun, a knife and a light axe. Making his own shelters. Living off the land – game, and wild fruits and greens. Somehow, in the mood I was in, this seized upon my imagination. Here was the ultimate in living. Back to basics. Dependent upon no other. Where money meant nothing. And there was the challenge.

His stories of living in the wilderness struck a chord. For here, basically, was the reason why I had returned to the countryside. I needed a simple life. One of the most interesting people I have ever met in my later life was an Indian professor guest of mine who summed it up pretty well. 'Europeans,' he said, 'accumulate too many – ' he fumbled for a word, waving his arms around the room at my furniture, radio, and general bric-à-brac, – 'Things,' he said. 'And pretend they are necessities. You Europeans are obsessed with Things. Your logic is obscured by the thoughts of Things. You no longer know the meaning of simplicity. And as truth is pure simplicity you can hardly recognize it. To find truth you need to give up every Thing. Truth is brought to the world by lonely men living simply in the wilderness.'

I needed, I suppose, to find the truth. Not a world-shattering truth about humanity. But the truth about myself. I had to try to find my identity, if I had one at all. Find a starting point.

But there was also the challenge, the adventure. Most of us have thrilled to the triumphs of Robinson Crusoe and the Swiss

Family Robinson. A desert island. Alone with perhaps just a knife and the clothes you stand up in.

I asked my companion how he had made shelter for himself in the backwoods. He was quite precise.

'First,' he said, 'you need what I call the "backwoodsman's eye" for the right spot. If you look around you can often find a shelter half built. Ideally it's a half-fallen tree, jammed into a neighbour with its trunk resting at an angle. You move under the trunk with your axe, cutting away the branches from the immediate underside but leaving the side members. This gives you a kind of tree-cave, and all you've to do is to build up the gaps in the walls using other branches, hard-packed fern fronds, or turfs. You start thatching from the bottom and working up, making sure that each layer overlaps the lower by a third; and that the walls are sloping at an angle *greater* than forty-five degrees. That's very important indeed. It's the whole secret – steep angles to turn the rain, and a damn good capping on the ridge, and no skimping of material. A nice layer or two of fir branches inside for your bed; and there you are. Dry and snug.'

He talked on about hunting and trapping, fire-making by friction, bears and moose, and big salmon that jumped into your arms, and furs and blankets; and canoes; and how to find one's direction; and dogs and rifles; and as time passed – about strange happenings and flesh-creeping unexplainables.

Then at last, with reluctance, he left the fireside and left the hut. I saw his torch receding down the track to the road. An owl called, a log stirred and set up a flare of light which animated for a moment the glassy eyes of the fox masks on the walls. It was quite a while before I summoned up the energy and inclination to undress and climb into bed.

To dream. To dream of an endless wilderness, creeks and mountains and forest. By morning it had become a desert island; and our own island in the 'allers'. A resolve was born – to live, for a time at least, on my own desert island in a shelter of my own building.

7 *The Shelter*

I had to decide what was basic if I was to live a Robinson
Crusoe existence for a time. Clothing – what I normally wore,
plus a few spares. A blanket or two for sleeping. I ruled out a
ground sheet to keep off ground damp. I would have to make do
with a thick carpet of birch twigs and bracken. Tools – one
knife and a light axe. Cooking utensils, after a deal of thought –
one tin can. When I discussed this with the Major later (he did
not bat an eyelid at the thought of my peculiar scheme), he
advised me to add matches to the list.

'You'll never learn to light fires by friction in time in a damp area like this,' he said.

Food needed some thought. I had access to a friend's small library of books on natural history, and I was lucky enough to find some reference in it to edible plants, vegetables and seeds, fruits and fungi. By the fire in the dark evenings I learned that surprisingly little, botanically, is poisonous in Britain. Quite a lot is edible.

It was interesting to learn that one of the most sinister families is the *Solanaceae* – the nightshades. The Deadly Nightshade and the evil looking and evil smelling Henbane; and, common in our wood, the Bittersweet or Woody Nightshade. Woody Nightshade to me is an attractive plant. Somehow, with its little purple and yellow flowers, strangely exotic. The Thorn Apple, of ill repute, is another member of the family. A strange one this, one year fairly common, then scarce, then after seeds having lain dormant for a long time, common again. It contains atropine and hyoscine, which dilate the pupils of the eyes and cause hallucinations. It was the ingredient of many a witch's brew in medieval times.

The *Solanaceae* – a sinister family. Yet is it? One of the family is a staple food – the potato. Its resemblance to the Woody Nightshade is fairly obvious. Another member is the tomato. The Woody Nightshade again bears a resemblance. The rough fleshy stems of potato and tomato are both uncomfortable to the touch. Leaves, flowers and fruits have similarities. Yet the carefully developed swollen root of the potato is edible and nutritious, and its fruit poisonous. The carefully tended fruit of the tomato is edible and nutritious, and the root poisonous. Who were the brave men who experimented with these two members of the *Solanaceae* to decide which of which was edible?

There are, of course, obvious plants to avoid. Hemlock is one. After reading the account of the death of Socrates I had imagined Hemlock to be an exotic, sinister-looking plant. In fact it is not uncommon and is one of the *Umbelliferae* family – the hogweeds – with crowns of white and off-white flowers that grow thick in the hedgrows and waste places. It is distinguished from the rest of the large family of rather common and uninteresting plants by its purple-spotted stems. Most of the *Umbelliferae* are useless weeds with unpleasant scents; yet not all are poisonous. Parsley belongs to the family, and caraway, and earth nut, and fennel and angelica. And carrots and parsnips and celery were developed from the weeds.

And here is one other member of the *Solanaceae* family which has played an increasing part in man's destiny and has lately been found to have its sinister side. Neither the root nor the fruit is used – only the leaf. It is the source of the comforting, and sometimes poisonous drug – nicotine. The tobacco plant.

I already knew a little about botany. My first aids to plant identification were the splendid series of cigarette cards which I collected as a young boy from packets lying in the urban gutters, or begged from passing smokers. Though I no longer have them I still have a vivid mental picture of them, and I still remember the joy of recognition of the first marsh marigolds, like great golden doubloons spilled about the water's edge. And the foxgloves, standing shoulder to shoulder like a purple army in the woodland glades. And the white perfumed foam of the meadowsweets; and, commonest about my childhood paths, the yarrow, a valuable herb, said my information. My grandfather once tried smoking the dried leaves of yarrow in his pipe as a substitute for tobacco as some recommend. He gave it up – but then he was a thick-twist man.

A neighbour of mine over the fell, a great horse man, also tried smoking yarrow over a long period and then suddenly gave up smoking altogether.

'It was like this,' he said, 'I had come to forget what tobacco tasted like, and I experimented with other dried herb leaves mixed in with the yarrow. Then one day I was smoking away at my pipe and thought, 'this is a rum do. Never had anything like the mixture before. Quite reasonable!' Then I found out by accident that my four-year-old lad had been stuffing the pipe with some dry horse dung. I sort of lost interest in smoking after that.'

Surprisingly few berries and nuts are poisonous, though many are unpalatable. Acorns used to be the peasants' starvation diet, and you would indeed need to be starving to stand their acidity. Far better to feed them to the pigs. Oak woods were a valuable part of earlier agricultural economy. Rowan berries, sloes, and wild cherries bring tears to your eyes if you try to eat them as they come. Junipers are sweet but strangely sharp at the same time, and rather oily. They were once used purely to spice food, and are used nowadays to give gin that sharp distinct flavour. Haws are rather tasteless and mushy, and hips are all kernel and seed and have to be boiled into submission. Elders are for drink makers; eaten raw the berries coat your tongue. Crab apple eaters need cast iron stomachs. Sweet chestnuts and beech often offer mock-seeds – mere empty shells. Only hazel can be relied upon to give a sound harvest of good food.

Raspberries, blackberries and bilberries offer the best hope of survival if you happen to be living in their season. Strawberries are plentiful in the Lake District but the wild fruit is so tiny that it takes an awfully long time to collect enough for a morsel, let alone a feast. If you have to rely on British plant food you will have a lean time of it. Watercress and bleached dandelion leaves are the commonest, but not very substantial.

The fungi of the British countryside offer no substantial wild larder either. I was again surprised, however, to learn that few are poisonous, and very few deadly. The deathcap is deadly indeed, more particularly so as it is similar in shape to a common mushroom, especially at the button stage. It could be, and has been, eaten by mistake. Stomach ache and sickness follow. After this there is a period when the victim feels rather better. It is as well if he uses this time to put his affairs in order, for death soon follows.

Another obvious fungus to avoid is the attractive red, white-spotted fly agaric. A morsel of this is enough to produce intoxication; rather more – hallucinations. The Vikings were reputed to nibble it before battle. It sent them berserk. The qualities of this fungus and its like are known the world over. Tiny quantities are deliberately added to intoxicants, including vodka.

It was quite clear that if a Briton was to survive for a while on his wild food, he had better make sure that he tried the experiment in the autumn when nuts, berries, and fungi are in abundance. Even then he would have to tighten his belt and put up with some stomach ache. Otherwise he would have to be a strict carnivore.

Unfortunately for my experiment I have a strong aversion to killing. I have had to kill for food before, but have hated doing it, though I have killed many suffering creatures as an act of compassion; a stern and distasteful duty.

It is not easy to explain the aversion. I could say that I am keenly aware that the life force is all about me and I am part of it. I tread on life whenever I move. I take in legions of tiny particles of life every time I breathe. Bright green life invades my eyes; the rustling, murmuring, whistling sound of life my ears; the rich moist smell of life is in my nostrils. Life cells flow through my body, living and dying. The great urgent force, the magnificent dance of life in all its countless forms, is such a vital and everlasting wonder to me, that personally to take away life from any wild creature diminishes my own.

I could explain all that. But there is the unclean brutality of the death blow, the last struggles, and the last look in the creature's eyes.

No. My Robinson Crusoe experiment would demand some bought food supplies. But I would keep them basic. Flour, eggs, potatoes, milk, and occasional fresh meat. But I could do without all the cooking paraphernalia. I could roast and bake without utensils. I would need just one tin can for boiling, brewing, and stewing.

I would allow myself a few luxuries – a candle or two, a few books, paper and pencil.

The first signs of spring began to approach. Alder and hazel catkins smoked yellow pollen. The frogs were creating a frenzied racket in the half-frozen ponds. Coltsfoot gilded the roadside banks, and the cock blackbird near my hut sung his sad song to the setting sun. Time to act.

There was a lot of work to be done in the area of the alder swamp. Dave was off to join a planting gang and I would be on my own. It was an opportunity to try the experiment of living in my own shelter with only the basics.

The major had told me that a shelter could be built in an hour or so. It took me much much longer. I chose an old pitstead on the 'island'. It was a patch of bright green grass growing against the background gloom. At one end of it was an oak, forked about six feet up its trunk. I felled another oak so that it jammed its top in the fork. This was the ridge-pole of my hut. Having made the start, I gathered my basic belongings into a haversack and moved to the site.

First I cut more wood to build up the sides – at an angle greater than forty-five degrees. I packed them close together. Then came the back-breaking task of cutting turfs. At first I did this with my clasp knife, then I found this to be far too slow and started to pull it away with my bare hands. It took a lot of turfs to cover that roof, and good turf is hard to come by in woodland, and full of wiry rootlets. Best place to lift from was from rock slabs where the roots could take no hold of the ground, and the turfs would peel off easily in one piece. Time flew on. I was surprised how fast; I was wandering farther and farther away for turf, my back and leg muscles were crying for mercy, and my fingers were sore.

Darkness was approaching by the time I was putting an extra thick layer over my ridge pole – and worse still, it was beginning to rain. I had no time to admire my work when I had finished it. I got a fire going not far from the shelter entrance, washed my hands in the stream, mixed some dough, and coiled it round a stick to bake it. Here I must confess to the one fraud. The only tin I had been able to find for a cooking pot was full of stew. I put this by the fire to heat up. I deserved one luxury.

It was raining hard by the time my meal was ready and I retreated into the black pit of my shelter, praying that it would 'turn the wet'. In fact it seemed to be doing this very well. Not a drop came through. After I had lit a candle and begun my meal, however, I discovered that there had been one possible mistake.

The grass side of the turfs might have been better inside. I had faced the roof with roots downwards, and lumps of soil occasionally plopped down on to my food, or down my neck, accompanied by the occasional small worm, or beetle. Still one had to enter into the spirit of the thing. Crusoe would not have bothered with such trifles. Here I was, in my own shelter, alone with nature.

Alone as pitch darkness descended. The fire was a comfort – until the rain put it out. I unrolled my blankets and turned in. I stared for a time at the candle flame. One tiny spot of light in the great cloak of darkness. Then I pulled out a Sherlock Holmes book and I was soon far away in Baker Street – until I found my eyes closing with utter weariness.

I do not know how long I slept, but I remember waking later in a panic, forgetting where I was and imagining that I had been buried alive, the smell of raw earth was so overpowering. The only sound was the falling rain, and the running water in the beck.

I fell asleep again, and I suppose this time I slept much longer; until I awoke in a far worse state with that rare, uncomfortable feeling of terror. The hair was moving on my scalp. My heart was pounding. Some noise had awakened me – an unusual noise. I lay waiting, with staring apprehension, for its repetition. It had stopped raining. The trees still dripped. The beck ran. But there was nothing else and time seemed to drag on.

Then it came again and I almost cried out in fright. A loud, asthmatical cough. In the stupor of exhausted half-wakefulness it seemed to me that out there in the darkness was a huge man – or a monster – or a thing. It coughed again, an earsplitting thunder of a cough. I gritted my teeth to stop them chattering and I heard heavy footsteps slowly sucking through the swamp nearby. I could hear it breathing heavily now as it snapped away dead birch saplings. Probably, I thought in fuddled confusion, it was choosing some club to pulverize me with. The wood broke like rifle shots! The thing had colossal strength! It coughed again, then blundered heavily about for a while. Then came utter silence.

I waited and waited, in blind fear, for more sounds. Unconsciously some instinct of preservation had directed my fingers to loosening my body from the pinioned blankets so that I could break out and make my escape if the attack came. Supposing it was to come at me and beat down my ridge pole! I would be trapped and buried alive. Suffocation was a recurring nightmare, but this was for real. I was very much awake. And time dragged on in silence. Although I tried not to, I thought of all the tales that I had heard about the wood. The thicket, for instance, where it was said (though I had never previously believed it) that the hounds from the local hunt would refuse to enter; for something in there struck them with terror. Perhaps this was the place! But there was only silence. Gradually weariness overcame my terror. Without realizing it I dropped off to sleep.

I awoke in daylight. Bright daylight. I had overslept. The sun, streaming through the new-breaking alder leaves outside, made their greenness blindingly fluorescent in contrast to the darkness of my shelter. My mind was still fresh with the terror of the night before as I crawled out. But sunshine has a wonderfully therapeutic effect on nerves. There was nothing in sight but trees, and no sound but the song of a distant robin. It was very reassuring and I could even give way to some reasoned speculation. I could rule out thoughts of nightmares. The reality of the situation was very fresh. 'Footprints,' I thought, 'I must check for footprints!'

I went down with some excitement, and a little apprehension, to the swamp. Then I laughed aloud with surprised relief.

I had not had the sense to realize that I had built my shelter only yards away from a mud-hole which any idiot could see was not natural. It was a deer wallow. My visitor, by the looks of his tracks and the height that branches had been snapped off nearby trees, had been a large adult stag. The same one that I had seen on my first exploration? He was travelling along his favourite trails, no doubt. Because of the overpowering smell of fresh earth from my shelter, his sensitive nostrils had at first not picked up the feared human smell. Deer have their favourite places, and their favourite routes. I was in the middle of one.

A good cold wash did me a power of good. A ham and egg breakfast – egg baked in the fire embers and ham on a stick – and I was off to work.

I lived there for a fortnight, and for odd occasions afterwards whenever I was working in that area. There was no question of 'roughing it'. The shelter turned back the worst weather. My meals were none the worse for not having cooking utensils. I got quite accustomed to cooking my meat in a trench lined with stones heated in the fire, covering it with more hot stones, and then sods and soil. I ate baked eggs and potatoes, baked twists of bread and, as the season went on, gathered raspberries and strawberries for dessert. I found wild watercress growing in a stream a little way up the nearby fell, and made cold meat and egg salads with it, mixed with bleached dandelion leaves and garnished with young leaves of jack-by-the-hedge, salad burnett and wood sorrel. Fresh spring herbs are fine. Too many experimenters make the mistake of using mature, high-summer leaves. I had no tea and tried several substitutes. One was to make an infusion of young holly leaves. I cannot say that it was a great success, but it was certainly stimulating and more satisfying than some of the stuff passing for tea that one buys nowadays.

The basics did not include soap. I had read somewhere, however, that white wood ash was a good substitute. It was better than nothing for ordinary ablutions; but for washing through my few clothes it was not a success. After failing at attempts to get clothing clean by rubbing, I decided to use the less sophisticated method of working in the stream and hitting the clothing with rocks. After all, this is the usual way of doing it in many countries, and it seemed to work. The first time I brought the stone down on the clothing I was showered very liberally, and afterwards found it was easier to wash and bathe at the same time. After several wash days I got the hang of it; though one could hardly say that my whites were whiter than white. Then one day, in an enthusiastic mood, I brought the stone down hard on to clothing on what one might call the anvil stone, and I left one finger in the way. Any lost soul who might have witnessed me at that moment, as I yelled and war-danced, half naked, on the beck bank, would think I had turned my back on civilization for ever.

I could not shave, and the makeshift wooden comb was not that good, so it was perhaps as well I had no mirror either in that first fortnight.

The stag never came back, though it was common to hear roe deer barking in the swamp. And one morning I awoke to find two pairs of startled eyes staring in at me from the sunny clearing. It was a roe buck and doe, alerted by my movement in the gloom of my tree cave. We stared at each other for quite a while until the two deer, satisfied with no further movement on my part, browsed their way out of the clearing.

Every morning there was a surprise awakening. Looking out into the bright green light, from the gloom of my shelter, was like looking from the black everlasting pit into paradise. Drops of dew catching the light at the tips of the hanging grass-thatch seemed alive, each with its own jewel-fire. This one brilliant mauve. This one red, or orange or bright dazzling green. Each one in isolation seemed to have vital cosmic significance as it hung there in the silence. Peering through the perpetual night of my room, the dew drops were bright stars in a galaxy stretching into a hazy green infinity. And time stopped.

There is a level of consciousness between sleeping and fully wakening when the worries of the day have not settled upon us; the body is stilled, and the senses wholly receptive. If the sun is bright, there is pure silence, or the birds are beginning to sing, this shining level of consciousness can come to be the nearest we will get to paradise this side of our quietus. Every day should begin so. This is no dream. This is the reality. The world outside is beautiful. We do our best to hide it. We cover it. We push it farther back. The ugliness we make ourselves. We originate our own worries. We put on our own shackles; build our own prisons. We can only glimpse the golden reality, briefly, through our tiny barred windows.

The days began so well so many times in my shelter; and I crawled through a jewelled doorway into a new morning.

Rain? Of course some days it rained. The light was subdued and the birds were quiet. But looking through the darkness of the shelter the light was still welcoming, and rain, in my small clearing, was not allowed a direct assault. It came through the defences of the tree tops, and was only permitted to drop leaf by leaf, twig by twig, gently to the green floor. And there was a delicious moment when I could savour a pattern and a music in it before facing the chill necessity of having to get out and endure immersion.

The business of the day was usually brought to my awakening notice by my only regular visitor – a tiny wren – who would materialize. He certainly never seemed to fly in. One moment he was not there; next he was; clinging to the grass roots at the entrance then working inwards, regardless of my presence, scattering earth crumbs and making quick little darts in the search for minute insects. A tiny brown frenzy of life, soul mate, a scarcher in dark places. Normally one only glimpses this tiny timid bird, which rejoices in such a long delicious Latin name, *Troglodytes troglodytes troglodytes*, as it dives into the hedge bottom. But this one came in so close that I could see every feather move. I could even make out facial expressions of curiosity, caution, discovery. I could see its bright little eyes peering into each corner.

The shelter was to be my home for periods for quite a while, and looking back I can remember no real discomfort. There were frustrations when cooking went wrong, but no dull moment. I suppose there was no time for boredom. Living with only the basics needs working at – very hard.

8 *Fire*

Spring in the Lake District can be as unpredictable as in any other part of Britain – only more so. One day may be perfection; with a warm sun and the whole world singing with joy and ready for the green explosion of new life. A day or two later the mountain rescue teams may be out in force looking for some luckless, and most probably clueless, walkers lost in a blizzard.

But May is often very good. By the middle of the month one

can be enjoying summer and walking through the new green woods without the torment of midges and flies that hang their fire until the coming of the tourist season. That year it was very good and it was fine to be alive.

The eventful day came in the middle of the month. The first tourists had begun to arrive. We had had quite a spell of dry weather. Last year's bracken was as dry and crisp as cornflakes, and we had had fire patrols out in the forest for some time. I was at the hut having breakfast. It was a fine morning but rather cool, the sky was egg-shell blue with wisps of high, sun-tinted cloud. There was a breeze blowing from the south east.

I was on my first slice of toast when I heard the frantic sounding of a car horn on the nearby lane. I cursed and wondered who on earth was acting the fool, and walked from the hut to the end of the little wooded plateau where I could have a view of the road.

It was Dave, in his father's almost clapped-out ex-war-department pickup.

'Drop everything and come on lad!' he called. 'There's a fire at the crossroads corner! Wood's alight!'

I ran back, grabbed a shovel, then scrambled down the bank. Dave had old Bill, another neighbour, with him, and I climbed in the back. Before I could sit, the car was off and I was in an undignified heap on the floor and scrabbling about for something to hold onto. The vehicle took the corners of the lane almost on two wheels and I hung on frantically. Before we had gone far I could smell smoke – bracken and gorse. I never smell it now without recalling the anger, and the panic, of that day. It had caught our wood! Our wood on fire!

To our right, on the other side of the lane from the wood – the eastern side – the fell was burning madly. Dave drove on past it. The fell was only bracken and gorse and a few birch. The sheep could run for it. It was the wood we were worried about.

By the crossroads the wide verges were black. The fire had crossed the road and the birches inside the wood were like torches, and God only knew how far the fire had gone into the interior.

The crossroads were at our northern boundary. Looking back one can see that this was very fortunate. If the fell fire had started farther south and crossed the road at that point, the whole wood could have caught light. This once very nearly happened, when a farm hand, burning gorse on the fell close to the middle of our eastern boundary, allowed the fire to get out of control. Luckily the only damage had been to some larch on his side of the wall. On this occasion the wind was blowing the fire across the north east corner. It was this that was alight.

Dave called, 'To the break by the beck! We should stop it there. There's some more lads coming and we called the brigade!'

Old Bill and I scrambled over the wall and Dave stopped back to brief a party who were just careering down on us in a carrier's lorry. We led the party through the blackened, and still hot scrub, and through the charred remains of young Norway spruce. We were running then, round the southern end of the outbreak. Dave called out something and a number of the party at the rear started beating forward. Dave caught up with our group near the beck and we started beating in from there. The fire was making a terrible racket. It was terrifying, hot, choking. There is hardly anything more frightening than a fire out of control. It awakens a strange, primitive, instinctive fear.

I beat the dried grass in front of me. It took at least two strokes on the same spot to put it out. There was just no time to make too sure. The rest of the line was beating forward and it was essential to keep up with them. I had to watch them on either side, and there were occasional moments of panic, I cannot say how long they lasted, when I thought that they were not working close enough to me and my stint was too large to cope with. All I could do was beat away faster like a frantic madman.

'It isn't so bad, lads,' I heard Dave call breathlessly. 'It's only – got this – corner. We can beat – it out to the wall – and save the rest. Hope that bloody brigade – can deal with the fell – before it jumps the road again!'

I can promise you that there is no harder job than beating back a fire. It is pure hell. Your lungs are crying out for air and being insulted by smarting smoke. Your heart is banging like a sledge-hammer, and your arms flaying up and down like a machine. You are tormented with the constant anxiety about keeping up with the others, and you curse the flames that refuse to go out. They spit and snarl and dash at you, and you curse back heartily and steadily, remembering all the naval expletives that you thought had been lost on demobilization day. The fire strikes back at you with blows of choking heat. As you think you are winning, and morale flickers up one notch, you glimpse, through the corner of your streaming eyes, that somehow the inferno has crept on behind you. Someone calls out and you shift back like a madman, and although every muscle, the heart and the lungs, cry out that you can do no more, miraculously you redouble efforts, turn about, and beat as if you have gone berserk. Then gradually you come to have no feelings at all. You can see only the great fires of Hades and the black shapes of mad, dancing men, on either side of you. Your brain has no control. There is a rushing noise in your cars. You have lost command of your feet and they shuffle and dance forward mechanically. Yet somehow, magically, impelled by some strange force unknown to you, your arms keep flaying up and down, up and down, up and down. It is as if your limbs are convulsed by some screaming lunacy. You are the victim of some primeval instinct of self-preservation. It is the same blind force that seizes upon a man in the heat of a close-fought battle. It impels him to superhuman deeds of bravery – or sub-human cruelty. It is the demon that lurks and awaits his cue, down, down in some deep recess of the human soul.

But we were slowly winning. It was not apparent at first. There were cries all about me as my arms flayed up and down, up and down. 'Watch that behind!' 'Close up for God's sake!' 'You and you – back here quick!' 'Come on over here!' But the angry racket of the fire was not as loud. Eventually, after I do not know how long, for time had now no meaning, someone called 'The wall!' and I could see the stone wall of the northern boundary on my left. The battle line, still fighting madly, had stopped its sideways movement, and we had a direct confrontation with a hot, but now narrow, band of fire that had consumed all behind it. The attacking fire line broke through once, twice, but was soon contained again. The anger went out of it and soon the flames were nearly all out. We were back into the charred remnants and working ourselves out of a job. At long last I stopped my flaying arms and looked around. Men had materialized from nowhere. They were all hot, and black, and absolutely worn out. I recognized among them a local farmer; the bottled-gas delivery man; the local vet; a retired army officer; and at the far end there was a group of scouts. There was a lot of noise in the distant lane which one could guess was from the fire brigade. We moved about, putting out red embers here and there and beating hard again wherever we saw smoke. Then someone was calling us from the lane.

The fell was really alight, but the strong wind had taken it to another lane at its northern end. Luckily the lane was above the fell fields at this point and there was a tall retaining wall. The fire was trapped there and was now spreading only slowly against the wind. We all crossed the wall and joined the brigade, who had exhausted their 'first aid' water supply, had given up trying to get water out of the shallow beck, and were beating up the fell. There was a collection of vehicles all over the lane, and someone was throwing out more shovels from the back of a lorry.

We climbed the wall and moved on up. This time the job was easier. We had our backs to the wind and it was helping us, blowing the fire away. There were also more of us. We had only to surround the fire's creeping against-the-wind attacking points, and we had it. We had only to concentrate on a clump of blazing gorse, then this gave out. Someone called, 'All right, boys. We've cracked it,' and there was a feeble cheer.

The brigade stayed on the fell and the motley army began to disperse. Dave and I and one or two others went back into the wood. We had effectively lost, I suppose, only about ten acres. It was now a nasty black mess of smouldering columns and stumps. I mourned the loss of one fine old pine. An old friend. Dave began organizing a make-safe party. I excused myself with a promise that I would return later in the day, and in the evening too if necessary. I was whacked.

I scrounged a lift back on the pillion of a motor-cycle, and staggered back up the hill to the hut, still carrying my blackened shovel. I suppose it was now about mid-day. I was too tired to check. I recoiled in horror at the sight of myself in the mirror. My face was black. I had lost my eyebrows and the front of my hair, and my eyes were sore and red.

First of all I drank a lot of pure, clear, cold well water, and put more water in pans on the gas rings. I washed my hands and ate a slab of cheese and bread. Then I stripped off my stinking clothing and had a good wash in warm water. I was surprised to find two ugly bruises on my right leg. I could not remember how I had got them and gave up trying. I had also a burn on my right wrist. There were burn holes, I discovered later, in my shirt and vest.

I took out some blankets to the warm bank on the lee side of the hut and lay down to rest with a book. I awoke with surprise what seemed like five minutes later. In fact about two hours had passed. The book lay at my side at the place I had opened it. I had then a touch of conscience about leaving the gang at the scene of the fire. I made myself a cup of tea, then got the bicycle out and pushed it up the lane.

When I arrived at the crossroads there were still one or two fire brigade members out on the fell. Dave and the men had gone. I walked around and satisfied myself that all was out. The wood around the fired area was wet. Somehow the fire brigade must have managed to get the hoses to water.

It was some days later when I was told how the fire had started. A picnic party the previous weekend had lit a fire under a pine tree at a favourite view point lay-by in the road. A local farmer had advised them to put it out. They had not made a good job of it, as the fire had smouldered away deep into the pine needles and peat surrounding the tree and had spread over several days, half underground, to the fell. A freshening breeze on the night before the fire had taken it into bracken and heather. I wondered if they ever knew what panic and damage they had caused.

9   *The Waif*

My diary for that year tells me the date was the twenty-sixth of
May. It had been a fine day and I had spent it, for a change,
climbing with some friends near Coniston. On returning rather
tired to my hut in the early evening I was surprised to see a
group of four boys of about twelve waiting for me there. They
were not known to me, and they were obviously from the camp
site. One of them was holding a bundle but I took no particular
note of it.

'Hello,' I said. 'Looking for me?'

'We were told to come to you,' replied the ginger-haired one.

'Well then, what's your problem?'

They shuffled shyly, then Ginger pointed to the freckled one who was holding the bundle.

'We found this near our camp site,' said Freckles.

My heart sank. Another injured bird, no doubt. I should have known. It was known locally that 'the man at the hut in the Great Wood' knew about 'animals and things'. They all came my way – an elephant hawk moth caterpillar (a fearsome-looking monster); a slow-worm minus tail; a dead stoat; a bird's egg; a young rat; a pipistrelle bat; and various birds.

'Well,' said a local man in the pub one evening, when I asked him why he sent his visitors to me, 'living in that jungle on your own – you must be a bit of a wild one yourself, eh? Have a packet of nuts, lad. They say you live on them up there.'

Birds were a problem. If it was just a case of exhaustion, that was not so bad. A rest and a feed in a warm cage a friend had knocked up was all that was necessary. Bad injuries meant 'the chop' (quietly, after the visitors had gone). A slight wing dislocation could be righted; but a serious wing injury, even if repaired successfully, made the recovered bird a slow semi-cripple. Slow birds get caught by predators. Slow birds-of-prey go hungry. It was a kindness to despatch them and it was a duty I hated.

'We think its mother lost it, or maybe left it,' said Freckles.

'Oh?' I said. 'Let's see.'

Then I cursed roundly and heartily under my breath. It was a tiny roe-deer fawn. It looked quite dead; but when I touched it, it was warm. It was perhaps two days old.

'Bring it indoors,' I said, trying to suppress my anger.

The solemn procession, Freckles at the front, shuffled uneasily into my room. I asked Freckles to put the fawn on the hearthrug. He put it down and it stayed in an untidy heap precisely in the way it was placed: body curved, long legs splayed out. Its eyes were almost closed, but the nostrils in its wide black muffle were just moving, and its tiny chest perceptibly stirring. It was play-acting dead instinctively.

One could not blame the children. They knew no better. It was the old story. If a small wild creature is found alone it is assumed that it is lost or abandoned for ever. One is overwhelmed with compassion for the pretty thing and it is picked up and fondled. It is often the kiss of death.

I told the boys that it was the practice of mother roe deer to hide the fawn in a bracken hiding place all day; she would come back occasionally to feed it, mainly at night. It was the safest thing to do, because the tiny fawn has no scent. Mother deer *does* have a scent, and enemies might follow that scent to the tiny offspring. The fawn knows what to do. Its speckled sides are perfect camouflage and so long as it stays in frozen stillness it can generally be passed without notice.

So this baby was *not* lost or abandoned; but now that they had handled it, even if they put it back where they found it, its mother would not recognize it, because it would bear the feared scent of humans. The fawn would starve.

I looked round at the round eyes of the boys. Freckles looked as if he was going to cry.

'What can we do?'

'Can you do anything, mister?'

I felt very tired suddenly. I told them I would have to have a think. I knew there were three possibilities. Firstly I could chance returning it to the place where it had been picked up – the boys explained where this was, quite well. Or secondly I could try feeding it with cow's milk – a very doubtful operation. Or thirdly – no, I decided not to tell them the thirdly. It was unthinkable. I would have to consider. And if they returned the next day I would tell them what I had done. They trooped off in silence.

The fawn remained motionless, as I cooked my meal and wondered what to do. By the time I had reached the coffee and discovered that I was well off for milk I had made the un-enthusiastic decision, and was soon trundling out the bicycle to borrow a rubber teat from the farm. I knew they kept a few for lambing time.

The fawn had not moved on my return, but I assumed it

would make a move once it became hungry, and I uncovered my typewriter and got on with some work.

As the evening drew on I saw some movement. It got its legs into a more comfortable position. Its eyes eventually opened fully and it lifted its head.

I put some milk to warm on the gas ring.

I then noticed that its legs were making convulsive efforts as it tried to struggle upright.

I filled the bottle and fitted the teat.

Its ears were now pricked and it was looking at me from its lying position with large liquid eyes. Its muffle twitched, perhaps at the smell of food.

After a noble struggle it got up, but it was trembling on those unbelievably long and spindly legs. It was a beautiful though fragile baby. It moved a step or two like a stilt walker on its tiny polished feet, then collapsed again in a ridiculous heap. It made two other attempts with the same result, but it was coming closer. Then it reached out towards the bottle, and I held it by its thin body and squeezed some of the milk from the teat into its mouth.

To my surprise, it took to the bottle at once and did not let go for some time. Its long-lashed eyelids were closed and it fed greedily. When it had had enough I helped it to the hearthrug, holding it by its bony shoulders as it stilt-walked back, and it flopped down there, rather more tidily than when it had been put down the first time.

So I was a reluctant parent. Some people keep animals for pleasure rather than companionship. I am not one of these. I like to watch wild animals, but I would never voluntarily keep a wild animal as a pet. The only other wild animal I have kept was a leveret that a dog had picked up. But he had the freedom of the place completely. He abused it at times when he took liberties with the meal table (he had a passion for warm tea), but eventually he went away as one might expect.

Wildness is absolute freedom. Attempts to domesticate wild animals often end in frustration and tragedy. They usually have to be caged, to be fed on unsuitable substitute food, and to be denied many of the natural activities that are prompted by their instincts. We do not understand the whole of their needs, for all the love and care we give them. We can seldom communicate with them as with a dog or a cat. Dedication, endless patience and a lot of time are called for. No one but an unfeeling person would devote so much to an animal, knowing that he must occasionally cause it some degree of suffering or frustration, merely for pleasure. I feel it would be morally wrong for gain.

So I had no illusions about keeping this roe-deer fawn. Although I was very surprised at the ease with which it had taken to the bottle, I had not too much hope for its survival. I confess, also, that I was not delighted at the prospect of some sleepless nights. But the die was cast. I made some feeding preparations for the night, cleaning out the bottles and, 'setting up stall' round the gas ring, turned in for the night.

That night I made my first new discovery about roe-deer fawns. I was deep in sleep with my alarm clock ticking near my pillow when I was suddenly out of bed, scared out of my drowsy wits, my hair on end and my flesh creeping. A fawn has a blood-curdling, high-pitched, ear-piercing, teeth-setting cry when it wants attention.

I lit the gas mantle. Was this the feeble creature that had flopped helplessly on my hearthrug some hour or two before? This animal which stood four square (well almost square) staring at me with its ears erect and its bright eyes shining in the gas light? It expanded its lungs with a gulp, and emptied them again in one burst of anguished protest. It was agony! I dived for the milk pan and lit the gas ring.

The initial fright, the torturing sound, and the feeding were repeated in the night thrice; and when the alarm clock finally went off in the morning, I hit the stop button so hard it made a hole in my hand.

When the children came round after breakfast the tiny speckled darling was a sweetly sleeping bundle on the hearthrug. I told them that I was feeding it, and I sent them to the farm for more milk.

I hung about the hut most of that day, but the roe slept until the evening, waking when I had put my own meal on the table, then shrieking for attention.

As I fed it I marvelled again at its beauty. The roe is the most attractive wild animal that we have. It has a delicacy and a soft roundness about its features. All deer are attractive, but most have a sturdier build than the roe, and sharper head shapes. Some are almost goat-like. A roe has not the slightest resemblance to a goat and I therefore never refer to its young as a kid. The deer experts (particularly the sporting kind who regard deer more as a gun target than anything else) call it a kid while it is with its mother, and thereafter until the following summer a yearling. It has been so decreed. In my ignorance I would not call a roe-deer fawn a kid, any more than I would call a Jack Russell puppy a kitten.

The fawn stood, legs apart, head lifted, eyes half closed as it sucked. It was perfect. Its speckled coat shone, and its tiny feet looked as if they had been treated with boot polish. Its upper parts were fawn coloured, darkening by the long ears. Its lower face and body were white, and there were large white speckles on its sides. These speckles are only on the fawn. They are lost later in the season.

Before turning in I again put everything handy for the evening feeds, and I was awakened in the same fiendish way four times.

On the evening of the third day I returned from the woods to find it awake and it came towards me as I opened the door, chest heaving and mouth open as it shrieked for food. After I had given it its fill it still seemed active so I walked out to see if it would follow. It came out, placing its feet carefully as if each movement required an effort of thought. I walked through the pines into a rocky part of the wood where there were hundreds of birch seedlings. It stopped at once and nibbled experimentally. I walked on, then turned round. The fawn suddenly noticed I was missing, saw me, then came forward at a confident pace. Inside one hour it had learned that leaves are interesting, and walking possible. The way it walked through the rough was fascinating. It could not push its way through some of the ground cover, so here it picked up each leg high, stepping over it, its knees coming up to chin height.

At a slow walk this method of high-stepping progress was almost ballet. If I moved away faster, compelling the fawn to do likewise, the movement was more ludicrous. It looked mechanical, like an old steam locomotive: all pistons and connecting rods. It was made all the more comical by the animal's ears-back expression of concentration.

It followed at my heels like a faithful dog. If I stopped, it stopped, looking about it, ears instinctively lifted to catch the noise that it supposed had alerted me. When at last I returned to the hut it followed me in, and when I sat down it took its place at the hearthrug. This was amazing. I had expected a great deal of difficulty in raising a baby of the wildest of our wild animals.

10 Escape

I was awakened again four times on that night, then looked out at one of those misty dawns that hold promise of a warm, bright day. I was bleary-eyed and drowsy but that optimistic feeling that comes of fine mornings and thoughts of a completely free day ahead, pulled me out of bed to the coffee pot and scrambled eggs.

The fawn was lying on the hearthrug but fully awake and alert. It followed readily when I went to the well for water and returned with me. A cold wash from the rain-water butt and I returned to find the pan reaching the boil, and soon the welcome smell of coffee.

After breakfast we walked out in the direction of the great crag. We took our time because the fawn was showing inquisitiveness. The way I had chosen was over a ridge covered in birch seedlings. The new leaves were bright green and the dew on them reflected the wakening sun. The fawn stopped among them and took a leaf into its mouth. It pulled back, then shook its head, breaking the leaf away and chewing. The tiny thing was trying to browse. There are no canine teeth in the mouth of a roe. The cropping is done by the lower incisors cutting against the gums of the upper mouth, and the mastication is done by the teeth in the cheeks. So the deer pulls back on the twigs it has chosen and tears the leaves away. The fawn was experimenting, and no doubt enjoying the taste. Then, and ever afterwards, it chose birch if it had a choice at all.

The choice was a happy one because birch grows everywhere. It is the colonizer. It grows on the quarry waste heaps in the Lake District before anything else. The birches of Borrowdale are famous. Few admiring visitors are aware that many of them are covering yesterday's industrial waste. Perhaps deer like birch leaves because their distant Ice-Age ancestors had to live on them. For the birch follows the retreating ice long before the oak can get a foothold. And the birch has a dwarf arctic form which is now very local in Britain, but which at one time must have been common and almost the staple diet of the early deer.

The fawn took only an experimental nibble at the alders and the new oak leaves, on the way, and presently we reached the summit plateau and I scaled the crag. The mountains broke into view first, shining new-green on their lower slopes and their sharp crags above looking particularly hard as their columns were picked out by the long morning shadows. Below, the lake appeared to be steaming as the mists evaporated in the warm sun. The bird song had been left below in the wood and we were alone in a silence which was eventually broken by a sharp cry above my head. A buzzard was hanging in the morning breeze, using the air like a toy, fondling it with its great wings, shaping patterns with its finger-like flight feathers; falling, soaring, turning, air-dancing for nothing but sheer joy. It was joined by another, slicing effortlessly through the blue sky, and the pair followed each other in a slow mating dance. I should say buzzard-watching is just about the perfect occupation for a lazy summer's day.

The fawn followed me as I jumped down the crag and plunged through the green coil-springs of newly opening bracken. It high-stepped its way with me when we left the plateau and through the rushes in a place known as Black Rabbit Well, and when we descended the slope beyond, it happened.

I had just stopped to allow the fawn to nibble at a low-hanging birch branch. It stopped feeding for a moment. I do not know quite what happened next, as I saw the fawn's sudden movement only out of the corner of my eye. But it was off. Running away from me.

I stood frozen with surprise for a few seconds and then I took off after it. It rushed through some scrub at an amazing speed and away into a swamp. I made good progress after it until I too hit the swamp and plunged in calf deep. The fawn was gaining ground as I fought with the black ooze, but I thrashed on. I went in up to my knees, but I swear that speed alone kept me from sinking further – that and the alder roots that I leaped for and sometimes reached. I was pretty sure that I was going to lose the fawn and my lungs were just about bursting, when surprisingly the animal turned out of the swamp and tried to scramble up a moss-covered outcrop. It stumbled and came down, and gave me the opportunity I needed. I lunged out and reached the rock just as the fawn was making another attempt at its summit. I grabbed it with a flying tackle and it gave one awful shriek that raised my goose flesh, and kicked and struggled like a mad thing in my hands. I pulled it to my chest and held on.

What was so horribly disturbing was the look of terror in the poor creature's eyes. They were glazed, and they looked at me without seeing me. It was the look of a helpless animal expecting the blow of death. A man can see nothing more degrading and shameful than that last look from living eyes stricken with hopeless fear. I was sick with some sort of disgust with myself as I breathlessly held on to the convulsed creature and carried it back to the hut. I spoke to it. I told it it was a fool. Could it not see that I was saving its life? By the time I had squelched my muddy way back to the hut it had gone limp, and when I put it on the hearthrug again it lay in an untidy heap as it had in its first hours with me. The only difference was that this time its mouth was open, its tongue lolling loose, and its chest heaving for air. We were back to square one. This time, I thought, it might well die.

I do not know whether or not I cared just then. This had been completely unexpected. I do not know why it had bolted. There had been no sudden movement on my part to startle it, for I had long ago learned that it is the quick and unpredictable move that produces the panic reaction from animals. I had taken care to do everything in the fawn's presence quietly and deliberately. Perhaps it was a scent in the air that spoke to its brief memory of its own mother's warm presence. Perhaps it had heard a call in the wind. I shall never know. But right then my hopes for its life were low and I cursed the day it had entered my life. I flung off my muddy clothing and cooled my temper with buckets of cold water.

It lay there for most of the day. When it stopped panting I had to feel for its heart to check that it was still alive. As it seemed as if it was going to survive, my hopes rose a little. What if I did have to start all over again? I knew the drill now, anyhow.

I decided to erect a pen for it behind the hut. I started and took great pains. I buried the corner posts deep and sledge-hammered in the rest. I nailed in two rolls of chicken wire, one above the other, and made a wicket gate of oak thinnings.

Late in the afternoon I was startled to hear the fawn calling for food. It was on its feet on the hearthrug and showing no signs of anything except hunger. I prepared a bottle, and it took the teat eagerly. It was a relief. The earlier panic might never have happened.

When it had finished I carried it out to the pen. I had thrown in some birch branches and it nibbled at these but could not tear off the leaves, because as it backed away with a morsel in its mouth, the branch followed it. I had to tie each branch to the netting. This did the trick, and everything was fine while I stayed in the pen with it, but as soon as I left and closed the gate, and it found that it could not follow me, it shrieked in misery. I thought I should have to be a bit hard and let it shriek for a while until it got used to the situation. That was no good at all. It started battering its tiny body against the wire, and falling about, and looking desperately frightened. I gave in and returned it to the hearthrug, and wondered what could happen next.

I had to feed it again in the night, four times. The following morning the boys who had brought this problem into my life turned up to see it. It obliged them by standing, then walking towards me; but as soon as one boy made a move it flopped down and looked at me nervously. I told the boy to keep quite still and it rose again and I got the tape measure and measured it. It stood fourteen inches high, and measured sixteen inches from nose to tail.

When the boys had gone I tried it again in the pen. This time I cut quite a pile of branches so that as well as providing browsing material they offered cover for it to hide away. It would not allow me to leave the pen without a noisy demonstration so I sat in with it while I prepared some vegetables for the evening meal. It tried and enjoyed the carrot parings I offered it; but quickly dropped the potato. It was not long before it discovered that the branches offered a hiding place and it settled down there. When I was sure it was asleep, I crept out.

All was well for the rest of the day. I went about my work quite sure that I had done the natural thing in offering, as its true mother would, a safe place to lie up and wait for its next feed. On my return it was in the same place but rose as soon as it saw me and rushed for the wire. I led it indoors.

I tried an experiment. Mrs C. had told me, when I had collected the milk, that if I dipped my finger in it and let the fawn suck it, then slowly brought the finger down into the bowl of milk, the fawn might learn to drink on its own. It worked the first time, though the drinking was noisy and clumsy. But I had to laugh when at last it raised its head, gasping, out of the nearly empty bowl, with its muffle white and dripping. The diary tells me that I was up to feed the fawn three times that night – but it was far less of a drudge using a bowl.

Its second day in the pen was a bad one. Whether its newfound method of feeding gave it indigestion I do not know, but it would not settle and it shrieked its objections. I let it out and it followed me down the lane to the farm. It caused a commotion in the farmyard. Some children staying there were brought out to see it, though I warned them from touching it: Tom pushed back his cap when he saw it and said 'Well, I'll be damned!' several times.

Milk and eggs collected, I led the fawn carefully home with an eye open for dogs. Our nearest neighbour had a spaniel bitch and it was sitting on the doorstep. I got ready to grab the fawn but the idle bitch merely strolled over suspiciously, sniffed at the deer, then walked warily back to its step. The fawn crowded me and stood still. I am quite sure that if it had run, and I had failed to grab it, the spaniel would have been after it. As it happened we were to have several encounters with that amiable beast and the response was always the same.

We had another encounter that day, too. Occasionally a very tame tortoiseshell cat would pay me a visit. I would find it suddenly, watching me from an outside window sill, or sitting on top of the porch, or peering in round the door. I did not encourage it beyond an odd saucer of milk. On this day it came in as the fawn was feeding from the bowl and watched it with great curiosity. The fawn looked up when it had finished feeding and regarded the newcomer without interest. The cat walked in very cautiously, then finished off the driblets of milk left in the bowl, and left as quietly as it came. From then on it became a regular visitor.

The great wood was now changing rapidly. It was never really the same from one week to the next. The bare late-winter prospect of transfixed columns, topped with a sky-scratching haze of twigs, had earlier turned green; and now the frenzied thrusting of shoot and leaf had closed in, shortening sight lines, and hundreds of impressions assaulted the eye. Distant sounds had gone, and the near-by hum of insects made one think of a saw mill. A hundred scents invaded my nostrils: bruised bracken; new birch leaf; bluebells; hawthorn blossom; the hogweeds which make me sneeze; the shock of crushed ramsons, the wild garlic; and the clean sweet smell of water mint.

As sight, sounds and scents closed in with the green walls, something had happened to distance. The walk to the great crag was apparently twice as far as at least. One walked now through crowded glades, pushing back curtains of leaves, and new grass and bracken pulled at one's feet, and fresh bramble tentacles snatched at clothing. Birds everywhere cried, 'My territory! My territory!', and every flower and hanging blossom said, 'Stay! Look!'

I took the fencing pliers, one or two larch stakes, and a sledge-hammer to repair an enclosure fence on the eastern side of the wood. The fawn came with me, picking its feet up high, muffle stretched up to pull at leaves, occasionally breaking into a clumsy run to keep up with me. I watched it carefully in case it was going to run for it again, but I was now apparently accepted.

When I reached the enclosure it browsed for a bit while I took out the rotten stakes, and then it settled down to rest in the new bracken, its speckled sides merging perfectly into the dappled light and the brownness of the old dead stems below. Dave came when I was hammering in the staples. I could hear him crashing and crackling towards us.

'Heard someone bashing away in here. Thought it must be you. Posts rotten, eh? It's the dampness, you know. Seeps in everywhere. That's why my brother Harry went to Australia, you know. The dampness got into his joints, he said. He said he expected his legs to snap off at the knees with the old rot. Needed hot sun.'

He sat down, put down the sickle and bag he was carrying, and lit a cigarette, carefully blowing out the match and pushing it into the ground. I estimated that the distance to the fawn from where he was sitting was about fifteen feet.

'Weeding?' I asked, nodding at the sickle.

'Round the bonny larches in my plantation. To be honest, though, I'm just walking around them watching them grow. If I hear anybody coming, I get out the old stone and give the blade a rub. Like the road men. They sit around on the roadside until they hear somebody then they get up and rub their hooks like mad. And the foreman, or the ratepayer, passing by thinks, "There's a true workman. Believes in keeping his tools well." You know, the council spends a mint on sickles and carborundums. Equivalent to a twopenny rate.'

I remarked on the speed that bracken grass and weeds grew at that time of year.

'What!' he said, 'Put your bait-bag down on a bare patch of ground, and at half-past twelve it's hidden under a foot of the stuff.'

It was good cover for game, I suggested.

'Oh aye,' he said, with a roguish look in his eye. 'I've known long grass hide a few games.'

I pretended to stare hard at the bracken to his right.

'What are you looking at?' he asked, peering in the same direction.

'A roe fawn. Unless I'm mistaken,' I said.

'You've better eyes than me, then. I can see nowt.'

'It could be some dead bracken. But I'm prepared to risk five bob. Bet you it is.'

Dave stared for a while, then said, 'You're on!' We got up and walked to the spot carefully. I parted the bracken.

'Dammit you're right,' gasped Dave. 'You have better eyes than me! Don't touch it, lad!'

'No', I said. 'Best leave it be.'

'Its twin'll be around somewhere,' suggested Dave. It was a

thought that had never previously occurred to me. Fawns are often dropped in pairs. Somewhere my fawn probably had a twin. And its mother would not be all that deprived.

'And its ma'll be around somewhere, too,' added Dave. 'And pa will be thrashing hell out of some young saplings. By George, it's pretty! Pity they grow up to be so destructive.'

I let the bracken fall back. Dave gave me five shillings. 'You have a good eye,' he said. 'I would never have seen it.'

Before he left he gave me a large piece of his sister's cake, and tore his coat on the raw edge of the wire netting.

It was more convenient to return to the hut for a late lunch by way of the lane. There was rarely traffic on it and I had no fear that the fawn might be scared out of its wits by vehicles.

On the way down the hill I saw a lady crossing the field on the other side of the road in front of me, and she climbed a gate on to the lane. She was carrying a bunch of newly-opened trollius. This garden plant, the globe flower, is very local and uncommon growing wild. But there was a large patch of it in a moist hollow in the field. She stopped short and her eyes opened wide when she saw the fawn following. She drew breath and stood stock still with amazement as we came closer.

She was holding the flowers down. The fawn approached her gingerly and nibbled a flower head. It obviously liked the taste for it continued on through the bunch, taking the yellow petals delicately, and not stopping until the poor young lady was just holding a bunch of stalks. She never said a word.

'I'm – sorry,' I said. There seemed nothing else to say.

'Oh, it's all right,' she said in a daze. 'I can pick some more. It's – it's the most beautiful thing I've ever ever seen. But nobody will believe this – '

I left her standing there, watching us with her eyes and her mouth still wide open as we made the gate.

'Beautiful. Nobody – nobody will believe – ' she was saying as we went through it.

I tried another experiment that night. Before turning in I brought in some birch and hazel branches in case the fawn

wanted to browse in the night. Recalling that it could not pull
off leaves unless the branches were held tight, I tied the
branches with string to every conceivable firm object – both
door handles; table legs; the cupboard door handles; window
latches. The effect looked vaguely like a church harvest festival,
though hardly as decorative. But as it happened, it was a
success. The fawn only shrieked twice that night and it was an
easy matter to warm the milk, fill the bowl, and climb back into
bed. I got used to the sound of rattling door handles, munching,
and the patter of tiny feet.

I had just finished tying the branches up when I was aware
that I was being watched. Dave was standing, gaping, at the door.

'I've been told all,' he said. 'Done by my best friend! After I've
inspected the beast you're coming with me to the Punch Bowl
and you'll be spending my five bob – at least.'

The next few days of parenthood were easier. For the two
following nights I was up to feed the fawn only once, and by
the second of June the morning and evening feeds were
sufficient, and it was browsing hard at the branches I brought
indoors. It accepted its pen more readily when the sun was well
up, but later that morning came with me on a much longer
walk. On examining it too, that day, I felt two hard lumps on its
head – the beginnings of a coronet. It was a buck, then, as I had
suspected, and I had to think of a name for it.

I had shirked the job previously. I could not give it a human
name. The neighbours had already called it Bambi; but I shrank
from the Disney whimsey. I decided finally that I could only
call it Buck. It was an easy name to call, and it sounded reason-
ably like the bark that roe make, not infrequently at some times
of year, when they try to locate each other or warn one another
of danger. In fact, on that same day that I felt the first signs of
its growing antlers, it tried to bark several times, very weakly,
when it drew towards feed time.

On the following day I witnessed the first sign of change in the
deer's behaviour. The tortoiseshell cat, contented after finishing
off its bowl of milk on the lawn, walked to the deer, tail erect,
and rubbed against his legs as he was browsing. Buck jumped a

few steps backwards very clumsily. I thought at first that he was scared, but to my amazement his head went down and he charged at the cat. The cat rolled over and retreated; but it was far too contented to be aggressive and made a playful move, claws extended, towards one of the fawn's back feet. Buck jumped sideways, and then shook his head, as a rabbit or a hare will do when at play, and he danced round the cat, which rolled over again and tried to grab a leg. This weird playful dance between a herbivore and a carnivore was a quite delightful and surprising sight. I rubbed my eyes. I felt it could not happen! The play ceased when the fawn's front feet came down on the cat's tail. This was too much for the cat. It made off.

The fawn-play continued from then on. It was a source of great joy to me, particularly as it always came as a surprise. It also meant that this wild creature was perfectly content, and full of the ecstatic happiness of healthy youth. He began to walk and run in the wood quite strongly. I would walk on well ahead and call 'Buck!', and he would leave his browsing and come on at a run. Then, for no apparent reason at all, on occasions he would halt, shake his head, at the same time prancing backwards, then stand feet wide apart with a strange, dizzy expression on his face. Then he would jump about, all four feet together, in a ridiculous manner; stop, shake his head again, whirl about; and then he would be away like the west wind on the fells. The first time he did it I thought that he had finally gone off wild; and that was it, because I could now never hope to catch him. But not so. He ran in a regular circle, pitching through thickets, side-stepping trees without touching a stem; leaping over obstacles. Faster and faster he would go in this play until I was almost as giddy as he with watching It was a wild, delirious scramble, more like flight than stride. He always ended with a leap at my feet, his sides heaving like bellows, breathlessly, and with a happy, complacent look about him which seemed to say, 'Did you see me? I can fly!'

I count those moments of watching fawn-play as some of the happiest in my life. I remember them now with a great deal of humility. For this creature that I accepted into my life with such heart-sinking reluctance, paid me back with measures of joy that I never deserved.

The play became a regular feature of our walks, and as he got stronger the speeds became faster and lasted longer. At mating time, it is true, roes run in circles in love-play – so persistently that a circle of bare ground is hammered out of the grass. But I had never previously heard of a fawn playing ring-o'-roses. This was something completely new to me, and so far as I know had not been witnessed by anyone else.

One day I put Buck to a test. It was an impulse on my part, and it was a stupid thing to do. We had walked through the wood to the great slab, and I selected the smoothest and most difficult part of it and began to climb. I reached the narrow perch twenty feet up that I had named Holly Crack because of a stunted holly bush that grew there, and I looked down. Buck was browsing happily below me and I called out 'Buck!' He saw me and came forward at a run. His feet scrabbled uselessly at the rock base and I laughed. Then Buck did a strange thing. He turned and ran back. I thought at first that he had got into some sort of panic, and was making off. He ran in a circle, and disappeared into some birches, then to my horror I saw that he was

coming back as fast as his legs could take him – right back to the rock face. In a flash I looked around, saw that the deer could only fall off if he came some way up the smooth incline towards me, and I also saw that I would fall off with him if I tried to grab him from where I was; so I threw one leg over the base of the holly bush and leaned downwards as the deer came up the crag – impelled by its great speed. He got to my level before he dropped on his front knees and began to slide down again. I leaned out and grabbed him by the shoulders. For a second or two we both hung there, off balance, as I struggled to pull him towards me. I succeeded at last and we were both perched, I very painfully, around the holly bush. I eventually decided that the only way off was to pull both legs to one side of the holly and then slide down the crag on my back, holding the fawn to my chest. We finished in an untidy breathless heap at the bottom. I cursed myself severely.

11   *Visitors*

Inevitably people got to know about Buck and we began to have visitors. This was often awkward, because they invariably came in the middle of the day when the fawn was usually not active. The gentleman from the local press was not very enthusiastic when Buck merely looked at him lazily from his day bed and refused to pose for his benefit.

I often wonder what really happened to another journalist who came without giving notice and thought that he had seen me but never did. I found out later that he had walked up my drive towards the hut and seen a man coming towards him. He knew that I lived alone in the wood, and perhaps he had been told by some quaint neighbours (if the first journalist's tale was anything to go by) that I had some strange power over birds and animals. He doubtless expected to meet an eccentric recluse. He did in a way; but it was not me. It was mad old Natty, walking towards him in bare feet like Moses himself, wearing the same old coat no doubt, tied round the waist with string, and carrying a large staff.

There followed what must have been the strangest interview that the poor journalist had ever conducted. Afterwards, he told the publican who had directed him to my place that he could get no sense out of me.

I had refused to show him the deer at first, and then apparently I had relented and taken him a long walk through the wood, muttering all the time. After walking through mud after me, and struggling under the weight of his camera for an hour (he said), it became obvious to him that he was being made a fool of and he told me so. I then turned nasty and threatened him with the staff and used some of the weirdest, most obscene, and sacrilegious oaths he had ever heard in his life. Eventually, by some miracle, he found himself climbing the wall on to the road, and was able to reach his car. I was stark, staring mad – and as for roe deer, it would not have surprised him if I had a couple of kangaroos and an alligator too. But so what? So had the nearest zoo.

A neighbour came round shortly afterwards and told me that a noted author-naturalist was to visit me around lunch time that day. He was, I was told, a skilled deer stalker and knew all there was to know about roe, but hoped to get some close-up photographs of the 'kid'.

'If he knows so much about deer,' I grumbled, 'why on earth does he intend coming in the middle of the day when all of them sleep?'

The neighbour was a bit surprised at my reaction, expecting a happier response at the prospect of the honour of a visit from the great man. I did in fact look forward to meeting the author, and prepared for his visit. Buck had settled down after his morn-ing feeds in the shade of some tall male ferns opposite the hut door. Rather than disturb him by putting him in the pen, I left him in the hope that he might be rested enough to put in some spirited movement at mid-day when the naturalist arrived. I cleaned the hut up smartly.

When the visitor did eventually come at about two o'clock, red-faced and serious, sweating in his smart tweed suit, camera on his shoulder, and followed by his cool and very smartly dressed lady, I welcomed him and told him how I had enjoyed his books. I invited them indoors and offered them coffee. They accepted it, while I was asked a few questions about the deer. He nodded at my answers like a polite headmaster. I glanced uneasily at his smart wife occasionally, wondering what she was thinking about my shabby home. But she was charming, and very enthusiastic over the bowl of wild flowers I had arranged for the occasion.

He would like some pictures, he said, for something he was writing. Where was the 'kid'? 'Follow me,' I said, and walked confidently to the male ferns. To my dismay there was no sign of Buck. I could not understand it. He was certainly there less than an hour ago, I assured my visitor, and we began a search while his wife sat on the slate seat near the hut door and waited. We searched everywhere around the hut. I called 'Buck!' I rattled his milk dish. We searched methodically, crossing and recrossing the green cover around the hut with the flies buzzing in the heat about our heads. Then we gave up.

I apologized profusely. Buck had never behaved like this before, I explained. Not to worry, I was told. They would call again in a few days' time. Dare I suggest, I asked, that they come in the morning or early evening? They agreed to come in the morning.

As soon as the sound of their car engine had faded into the distance, I again called 'Buck!' To my surprise he stood up within a few yards of me, in a clump of hazels, hunching his back and stretching lazily. How on earth we had missed seeing him I shall never know. We had certainly, I felt sure, looked into those hazels. Or had we? And anyhow, was not this the great deer stalker who knew all about roe?

'Buck,' I said, 'you ought to be ashamed of yourself! Damn you, you heard me call!' The fawn walked lazily into the hut and looked at the table hopefully for his new-found delicacy – bread; or better still cake, with fruit, particularly the kind Dave's sister made.

On the appointed morning the naturalist and his wife again arrived. This time he was dressed in light drill, like a white hunter. She was sensational in a pale dress with a full skirt and a large-brimmed summer hat, and she smelled of lavender. This time Buck was very much in evidence and enjoying browsing on fresh green birch branches I had put in his pen. I took them round and introduced him. Buck then behaved in a strange manner. When neighbours came he normally carried on in his easy captivating way, nibbling the flowers they offered and showing no signs of shyness. But this was the exception. He refused the flower head offered by the gracious lady and regarded her with suspicion. He would not stand where we wanted him to stand for the photograph. He watched the cameraman as if he was going to bolt for the fence at any moment. There was that strange, unusual, unhappy, half-glazed look in his eye that scared me. I spoke to him reassuringly. I was not getting through to him. We eventually got him to pose where we wanted him but he stood in a wooden manner, ears erect, and watched our movements closely.

The naturalist obviously knew all about the danger of making sudden movements, and he took great care in all that he did. His wife, too, must have been used to situations like this and remained quite still and spoke in whispers; but I wondered afterwards if in fact the fawn did not like the way the wind moved her full skirt? Or perhaps the lavender was too much for his sensitive nose?

The naturalist got his photographs, but it was hard work; and neither of us was very happy about them. The deer was too much on its guard, he admitted. Perhaps he would call again. Meanwhile, he would have the pictures developed and printed and would send me copies. He was not happy about his camera either. It was new and he had not quite got the hang of it. He was off to London for a time, but would write.

One evening I heard a timid knock at the open door as I was setting the table for my meal. To my surprise there was a young lady standing there, shy and embarrassed. At once I recognized her as the one who had been robbed of her bunch of flowers. She had brought a girl friend, an athletic-looking veterinary student, and could they please see the fawn? I told them to come in and sit down. They sat, very quietly, on the extreme edge of one of the oak benches, and looked at the snarling hunting trophies on the walls. I poured warm milk into Buck's bowl, put it down, and rattled it hard. There was a silence that you could cut with a knife for some seconds: then suddenly, like the startling rattle of an automatic weapon, Buck's feet scrabbled on to the wooden floor then stopped dead. He looked at the strangers, pushing his head forward and taking in their scent with his twitching black muffle. I told them to keep still. Reassured that they were harmless, he skipped to his bowl and buried his face in it. I heard the girls draw in breath. Buck made a passable imitation of a hungry pig and then lifted his dripping mouth from the bowl, gasping for air. There was a duet of 'Ohs!'.

'May we – touch him?' asked the bewitched flower girl. 'Gently,' I said, 'but don't stroke him.' People expect wild animals to respond to petting as domestic animals do. Animals cannot always understand that a stroke is a friendly gesture. Buck certainly always objected to a stroke by walking away backwards, later putting down his head in a defensive gesture. Brock, an amiable badger owned by a friend of mine, objected to stroking more violently; and if it chooses, a badger can bite to the bone.

The veterinary student asked a number of questions about feeding and about Buck's habits. The flower girl lifted the deer's head gently by its white chin and looked at its large, heavily-lashed eyes. She was enthralled. Buck tolerated this treatment for a while then decided to make off. We followed him out. The flower girl offered him a hazel leaf. I told her to hold the stalk tightly. He lifted up his head, sniffed at it carefully, decided it was young and fresh enough, tugged it into his mouth and chewed it slowly. He amused the girls by stopping half-way through the chewing to thrust up his ears and listen to a noise in the wood. The leaf dangled like a large green tongue. More leaves were thrust at him, including his favourite sorrel. The weed was very common about the hut. It has a sharp acid flavour beloved of deer. There was a duet of ecstasy. He behaved impeccably, then grew bored of the attention and moved away to the bank top. The girls said 'thank you', and the student made as if to go; but the flower girl was watching the spot where the spindly back legs and speckled body had vanished into the undergrowth. She was in a kind of trance. Her friend grinned at me and pulled her gently and firmly away.

Albert and Eric were unlikely inseparables – Albert was tall, slim, well-schooled, serious, and a civil servant; Eric, small, swarthy, ebullient, and a factory worker. In the city they lived in completely different circles. They might well even have passed each other unrecognized in the street. But the mountains brought them together every weekend and holiday. They made a perfect climbing partnership. Albert was very cautious, and worked out each move like a mathematical problem. Eric was enormously alert, and had just about the right amount of cheerful aggressiveness. Visits to the Lakes were made in between trips to Snowdonia, the Highlands, and the Alps. Sometimes, for a laugh perhaps, they took me out and brow-beat me up some beetling brow of high crags. They were firmly 'hooked' on mountains psychologically; and very often literally. Those who have not tasted the delights, the adventure, the discomfort, the challenge and sometimes the tragedy of the high hills, can never understand. But the utmost height of bliss is stepping along some sharp ridge in sunshine, wrapped around with a great blue sky, after climbing up out of that care-ridden fleapit of earth thousands of feet down there in the purple depths. I am just as firmly hooked on mountains, but that is not what this book is about.

The three of us had had a glorious day on the fells together. We had finished it off with one of those famous Lake District farmhouse teas, and I had invited them back to an evening meal. This was their first visit to the hut. They knew nothing about the deer. We walked from the lane, round through the pines. From this angle the pen could not be seen. I was a bit anxious as it was some time past Buck's feed time. But there was no sound. I told them to go in and sit down, put a flagon of cider and some glasses on the table, and went round and opened the pen gate. Buck stretched himself and to my disappointment walked past me and nibbled the sorrels on the grass bank. I returned to my friends.

They had been in all sorts of queer places, but perhaps nowhere like this hut before. Eric was running his fingers over the points of the teeth in the snarling jaws of the fox masks, and singing some hunting song that he had picked up, no doubt, at some local pub. Albert was sitting on an oak bench, arms folded, taking it all in. I organized the old stand-by, sausages and beans, and sawed some bread, and we fell to. Almost the only time Eric is silent is when he is eating. All was quiet, then, when Albert held up a fork and said, 'Listen!'

'What is it?' I asked.

'A noise outside,' he said, looking back through the open door. 'Nothing there though.'

'Some wild beast,' said Eric, 'out there in John's jungle.'

We carried on eating.

I have seen Albert and Eric face some bizarre situations without batting an eyelid. But they were completely unprepared for what they saw next. I noticed first that Eric's jaw had dropped open, half a sausage stuck on an immobile fork, as he stared hard at the doorway. Albert turned and was also frozen in a moment. I pretended not to notice and carried on eating.

Through the corner of my eye I saw Buck walk to the table edge by Albert's elbow. He stretched his neck and carefully, between his lips, removed the slice of bread that was resting on the edge of Albert's side plate, then walked out to eat it.

There were some seconds of silence, then Eric at last exploded, and I heard the deer, startled by the outburst, run away up the bank.

'What the – !' Eric was bellowing. 'A deer – !'

'What on earth are you babbling about?' I asked, looking at Eric with all the surprise I could muster.

'You saw it didn't you?'

'Saw what?'

'The deer, damn you! The deer!'

'What deer?'

'The thing that snatched Albert's bread!'

I looked with amazement at Albert.

His mouth was still open and he could say nothing. Oh, how I revelled in this situation! I remembered the many occasions when I had looked with similar horror, to my colleagues' amusement, at some seemingly unclimbable face. I savoured the moment as long as I could.

'Damn you, you must have seen it!' Eric was almost hysterical.

'Where?'

'It took Albert's bread!' His voice was almost falsetto now.

He made a gesture of appeal to Albert.

'A young deer, a fawn, came in – ' said Albert quietly.

I stared at them both with horror.

Eric could contain himself no longer; he flung down his sausage, grabbed me by my shoulders and rushed me outside with super-human strength. We both looked up the bank. Albert came out behind us. There was nothing in sight but undergrowth and trees. Eric began to rush about like a wild thing, beating the ferns, and running round the corners of the hut. I could contain myself no longer. I laughed and laughed until I collapsed.

They dragged the truth out of me at last, and later watched with amazement as the fawn came down for his milk. Eric's parting shot was, 'We'll pay you back, next time you come up the hill with us.'

My employer also paid us a visit. He was obviously not happy about the deer and I knew what he was thinking. 'In a couple of years, when it gets independent,' I said, 'it could be a problem; and its antlers like bayonets.' But he admitted that it would seem that I had had no choice in taking on its rearing. He asked me to take particular note of what it ate, as not a lot was known about deer diet. Other than that he regarded it as my problem; he didn't really want to know.

Some time later I got a letter from the author-naturalist. It contained some quite poor pictures. He was profuse with apologies. It was a new camera. He was now getting used to it and he would call again. His wife sent her kind regards, and she thanked me for my hospitality. I never saw them again.

12   Growing Up

If I left the wood for any period, I preferred that Buck should be in his pen. He would normally stay there without trouble so long as he had settled down well before I left, and provided that I moved away without hurry. If my departure was too swift he probably felt that I was retreating from danger, and his new-found instincts told him that it was time to run with his parent, as he was quite capable of doing. He was growing bigger and stronger. Four weeks after his arrival he had grown three inches higher and longer. After his morning feed, if I did not put him in his pen, he would find a hidden spot on the bank where he could watch my movements while being invisible himself. It was hardly ever the same place twice, so I could not really say at any moment where he could be found. He would come to a call; or if I ventured away from the hut he would be at my heels before I had gone very far. So if I shouldered a pick axe and went off to work in the wood he would come with me. Sometimes I would think that I had given him the slip, for I might go more than a hundred yards through the wood with no sign of him. Then I would look round and there he would be, browsing casually as he came along, never looking at me, or even towards me, but drifting along as if it was the most natural thing in the world.

If I was leaving the wood for only a short time I had the choice of penning him, or trying to give him the slip. It was not so easy to get away unnoticed. A roe's hearing is exceptional. Those long, mobile ears can pick up the sound of a crawling insect, and the ability to turn each erect ear independently means that the sound can be pin-pointed as surely as by radar. One heavy footfall, or a crackling twig, and the game is up. I managed it occasionally when I went off to collect the milk, but more often I failed. I would be well down the road, congratulating myself on my cunning, then I would turn around and he would be there, grazing on the grass verge as if he just happened to be fancying a few of the roadside weeds when I had arrived, and he might as well come along too to pass the time.

At night Buck continued to live indoors, and he needed more and more branches. Some time after dawn he would yell for breakfast. 'Roe-deer kids', the experts say, 'pipe'. That is the official term for their call. It is a farcical description of the high-pitched yell. It should be appreciated, too, that I had to endure it indoors, and because the fawn knew where I lay, it was delivered a matter of a few inches from my face: what politicians call an 'eye-ball to eye-ball confrontation'. I would open my heavy lids to find myself looking at a deer's head, ears erect, eyes bright, in close-up. And if I did not spring into instant action there would be a repetition of the ear-splitting pipe.

I eventually decided to try the experiment of leaving the door open one night. I overslept. There was no deer alarm clock. So that, I thought, was that. He had got himself lost. I went out and called him. Not a sign. I got dressed and walked into the wood and called again. Still no sign. So I returned for breakfast. I was not going to search on an empty stomach. At the marmalade stage his feet rattled on to the wooden floor and he was there, sides heaving for breath and muffle dilated as he gulped in air after a long run. I poured out his milk.

I tried the open door again intermittently, but he was always there in the morning when I awoke. I do not know what happened on that first night of freedom. Chased by a dog? Or just one of his headlong romps taking him farther away than he intended?

One of life's most difficult attainments is the establishment of satisfactory relationships with others. Even the closest friendships, while bringing great happiness, fall short of the perfection we crave. It is not possible to be close enough for long enough; to understand completely, or to be completely unselfish. A true rapport is a rare experience. It seems to me that one of the greatest, perhaps *the* greatest, object in life is to find and know ourselves. And afraid of what we might find and learn, we pretend that we see ourselves in the persons we most esteem. The qualities we would admire most in ourselves, we seek in others. If what we hope to find is great, and noble, and superhuman, we must find a god, and seek the highest communion.

The gods of the primitive races were animals. If a tribe wished to be brave in battle, its god and its badge might be the lion. If it craved to be strong and virile, it might choose the bull; noble and fleet of foot, the stag; fierce and stubborn, a wild boar or a bear; great and masterly, the eagle. Some tribal badges are still retained in the heraldic emblems of our old families.

Having adopted an animal god, the tribe would seek a relationship with it. They would follow it, and watch it, and emulate it. The chiefs might even dress in its skin.

A roe is not obvious tribal totem material, and no sensible

person would seek one out as a companion. Its greatest physical attribute is speed, and the ability to disappear. It usually prefers to avoid danger rather than stand and face it. Though no duffer, it is not notably intelligent. A family rather than a herd animal, like the horse, it has no instinctive loyalty to a leader, and one cannot expect obedience, or to teach it anything.

Those of its attributes which might appeal to a primitive tribe, are not on general display. It is no mean fighter. Bucks sometimes fight to the death for the favours of a doe. And hunters have sometimes been injured when they have been about to dispatch a wounded animal. The thrusting power of its hind legs is considerable, its dagger-like antlers are a fearful weapon. But it is not the obvious hero-type.

As Buck progressed, however, his play showed some of these fine characteristics. If I pressed on his forehead he would become instantly alert, and his expressive eyes would brighten as he warmed to the great pushing game, head well down and rear legs thrusting. If I was to give way only a little he would press home his advantage by bringing in the assistance of his forefeet, lifting each leg high and kicking back powerfully, the muscles impelled like pistons. If he lost the game and I pushed him into retreat he would suddenly disengage, leap aside and circle, but, with me at least, he would not return to the attack.

This aggressive play was also pressed upon the long-suffering tortoiseshell cat. The first time it happened I was sitting on the grass honing a bill-hook; Buck was standing browsing a few feet away. I looked up and was startled to see that the deer appeared to have grown to a considerable size. I then realized that this phenomenon was caused by his hair standing on end. The whitish hair which is thick about the rear-end of a roe, and which hides the tiny, almost non-existent tail, had also spread out fanwise. I wondered what on earth had caused this alarming transformation, then I saw that the cat, the poor unsuspecting creature, was approaching the deer with tail erect. She was met by a brutal charge that picked her up and threw her several feet away. Before she could recover from the shock of this outrage, Buck had bounced forward, jabbing with his front feet. The cat gave one yowl and shot up an oak tree. The surprise was then on Buck's part, the speed of the cat upwards had lost it to the deer's field of vision, and it stood, head very erect, ears moving to try to locate a sound. The cat said nothing, but its eyes blazed its indignation. Buck, apparently accepting philosophically that cats have the ability to disappear, recommenced grazing, and the hair on his back gradually returned to its normal lay.

Strangely, the cat bore no ill will, and later that day returned at the deer's feeding time for hand-outs without any sign of nervousness.

Although the attributes of the roe might not have been so obvious to the primitive tribe seeking an animal god, its supreme beauty has always been recognized. In the Song of Solomon, according to the King James translators, 'my beloved is like a roe'. A supreme compliment. If a lover were to describe a beloved in similar terms today, it would probably not be well received. For the roe nowadays is an unfamiliar creature. It hides in the fragmented remnants of the forest that once covered Britain. But long ago, when roe fed on the fringes of the villages, and at the gates of the cities, all would have wondered at the fairy-like beauty, and the smooth poetry of their moving. A fawn feeding among flowers in the haze of a sunny dew-wet dawn, through the foam of meadowsweet, pulling at the glowing coals of sorrel heads; each foot raised and placed with smooth elegance and precision; the movements of head and neck smooth, and flowing, and unhurried, is a wraith-like vision, the insubstantial stuff of dreams; such as one would expect to see only at the gates of heaven. How could the lover best describe the breasts of his beloved? In the Song of Solomon he reaches for the highest possible simile: 'Thy two breasts are like two young roes that are twins, which feed among the lilies.'

The roe can never be a loyal and obedient friend. Its instincts do not demand it. I was 'family' to Buck; he trusted me to provide some food and some protection. He would prefer that I would be around somewhere; as this huge, confusing world, loud with sounds, and heavy with strange scents, was rather menacing. I was security and reassurance, nothing else. On my

part I expected nothing from him. I had not sought his
company. I accepted the responsibility of caring for him; and I
was grateful for the daily visual feast of his presence. But he was
also giving me something else. I was beginning to move quietly.
This was partly in the first place because I had no wish to startle
him; but partly, through watching his movements, mine were
more precise. If Buck 'froze' in his tracks and his head came up
and his ears moved round, I would also stop dead and listen with
him. Sometimes the sound was so far away it was never
identified among the babble of familiar bird noise. But sometimes after a long wait the maker of the strange sound could be
picked out – a buzzard mewing above; a squirrel jerking his
way along the branches as if tugged by a string; a blackbird
excavating in the leaf litter; a cock-pheasant, trailing tail feathers in the old bracken. Because of Buck, I can hear a shrew in
the grass, I can hear butterfly wings; not because of particularly
sensitive hearing but because I am ready to receive these
sounds.

Once at such a moment of hypersensitivity, after seeing a
rabbit pass us, I saw Buck's muffle move and his hair begin to
rise. Both ears were trained towards a heap of earth, pulled out
by a fallen tree root. In a cavity in its side two wicked little eyes
stared towards us. For some time there was a three-sided staring
match. Then out of the roots slid the smooth undulations of an
insolent stoat. He moved towards the deer. Every hair raged on
Buck's back. The stoat's little eyes were turned towards me. He
was following the scent of his rabbit and nothing was going to
stop him. There was something so audacious about his manner
that my flesh crept too, then I reacted by picking up a clod and
hurling it at the beast. It ran back to the root and disappeared. I
picked up another clod and moved towards the root. I was then
startled to see the stoat reappear at the mound top at my eye
level. We stared at each other for a second then the stoat
opened his mouth, showed his rows of white teeth and actually
snarled at me. I aimed wildly and he was off like a brown flash. I
then sat down and laughed, while somewhere a frightened
rabbit was waiting for the bite of death that never came. Buck

was already browsing again, his hair slowly subsiding, and a frustrated stoat was waiting indignantly for our departure so that he could pick up the scent of another luckless bunny.

I have no dislike for the stoat. He is an efficient hunter and a quick killer, and but for him and his smaller cousin the weasel we would be overrun by rabbits. He is so efficient that once a rabbit knows that he has been singled out he often makes no strenuous efforts to escape. Sometimes you might see a rabbit staggering about as if drunk. Shortly afterwards you are certain to see the stoat's long sleek body undulating behind and hear the last squeal of the rabbit's breath. If you then fancy rabbit for dinner you should run towards the sound of the expiring creature, chase off the stoat, and you will have your rabbit neatly killed and practically unmarked – just the teeth marks in the throat. I have cheated quite a few stoats of their dinner in my time.

I have also seen, on one or two rare occasions, a stoat in winter ermine. Completely creamy-white except for the black tip to the tail, which is always present. Not all stoats change to winter wear. It is commoner in the north of Britain than the south.

There was another occasion on one of our walks when Buck stopped browsing and his hair rose again. The ears were pointing directly to the old timber trail ahead. I waited for what seemed a long time, then I saw the leaf litter moving. An adder was making a leisurely wavering track towards us. It was probably about two feet in length; then presently, at its tail, followed another, smaller specimen. They left the path to our right then paused on a rock slab, their little tongues feeling at the air. Buck then reacted very strangely. He jumped, four feet together, and moved forward as if he was prepared to attack with his sharp fore-feet. Like two pieces of elastic the snakes snapped into the grass and had gone.

A roe at rest is one of the most peaceable sights imaginable. He carefully treads out his resting place, folds his legs beneath him as precisely as all his other movements, then half closes his lids and brings up his cud. He masticates with leisurely enjoyment, like an old countryman smoking his evening pipe at his cottage door. He can keep this up for long periods, only stopping, for a moment at a time, when his ears, ever moving, pick up an unusual sound, and he must know what, in which direction, and how far, before he continues.

But deer watching is all right when there is little to do. When I had to go out I had sometimes somehow got to give him the slip. I had discovered that one method of stealthy exit from the hut, avoiding his observation, was by a back window. It called for a certain amount of physical agility. With a cunning hitch up out of the window I could climb on to the roof. I could then creep along the shingles to a corner and drop lightly into a carpet of pine needles. This was the side of the hut away from the deer's usual vantage point, and if I avoided dead leaves, dead twigs, and squelchy earth for at least a hundred yards, I was away. I was executing this difficult and highly suspicious looking manoeuvre along the roof one day when I was suddenly conscious that I was being watched. Dave was standing below with his mouth wide open.

'I knew it,' he said after a long stare. 'I knew that living alone in this place would eventually send you up the wall.'

I dropped down at his feet and made some appropriate remark about the weather, then tried to explain what I was trying to do. He shook his head sadly. 'What you need,' he said, 'is a complete break. Luckily that's why I'm here. It's Billy's twenty-first birthday, and as the lad's no family we're giving him a tatie-pot do at the Punch Bowl tonight. I'll be round for you at seven.'

13   Tatie Pot

If there is one great tradition in the Lake District that I cherish, it is the tatie pot. It is a glorious dish of mutton and potatoes with slices of black pudding, all in rich brown gravy. Nowadays some of the pubs' offerings in this line are somewhat indifferent; but the Punch Bowl was good. I looked forward to Dave calling for me.

I did not, however, look forward to the drive. Dave's van did not inspire confidence. It was a typical farmer's type. One started it by switching on and then pulling a wooden toggle dangling on the end of a piece of baler twine; the exhaust gases played tunes in the perforated exhaust pipe which heated the metal floor at your feet. The clutch came in with neck-breaking suddenness. The brakes were good, but Dave believed in using them frequently between aggressive jabs at the accelerator. The seats were hard, particularly the backs, which belted into you at every nerve-slamming jerk one way or the other. Invariably your door had to be secured to some point in the interior with string, 'to make sure'. The interior smelt of an indescribable mixture of petrol, exhaust, paraffin, creosote, and manure. I once found an egg on the seat. ('Blast that daft Rhodie,' grumbled Dave, 'it lays the damn things everywhere.')

I heard his horn sound dead on seven. I had already effected a successful deer-free escape from the hut, and was at the gate as he jerked round the corner. We were quickly away up the hill and down the hairpins at the other side. At the crossroads we picked up George, a hefty lad who 'wrastled' with the best, for the local sports still fostered Cumberland and Westmorland wrestling. George was red-faced and genial, and cheerfully crushed me against Dave's shoulder and the gear lever. We were off again. At the next lane end we picked up Stanley, a small, fair young man with untidy hair and wide open eyes, which gave him a constant expression of surprise. He climbed in the back and sat on the tool chest. Dave waited until he had shouted 'All right' before letting in the clutch.

We pulled up in the yard of the Punch Bowl just before Billy arrived. He was a long, lean, bony lad and he thundered in on a large motor bike to a welcoming cheer. He unwrapped himself from the controls, pushed the goggles up on to his cap, and took the birthday greeting with a stern face, and a nod. It took a while to get used to the fact that Billy's face was almost always expressionless. He laughed only with his pale blue eyes, and spoke seldom.

We got into the snug bar, lit by a log fire which shone on the polished stone floor, and the old smoothed oak beams and props. No wealthy brewery had yet taken it over and tarted it up. It looked like a farm kitchen and was just as homely. Mark, the landlord, was a hunting man, and the pictures on the walls were of hunts and hounds. There were one or two fox brushes and masks on the beams. Mark was big, smart, an ex-officer of the Royal Marines, and he sang a fine baritone. Betty, his cheerful red-haired daughter, who also served in the bar, was mad on ponies, and, so it was said, on Dave. Dave sometimes took her out, but was very non-committal about their relationship.

Mark served us that evening and we drank bitter and pulled Billy's leg, and told him that it was time he knew the facts of life. Billy was something of a philosopher.

'All tha needs to know,' he said, 'is that tha canna get a quart out of a pint pot; and that goes for tha wage packet, tha woman, or tha bodily strength. So m'grandfayder told me, and in twenty-wun years I've fund it. George there has a quart a body and a pint o'brains. He can thraw the best wrastler in Westmorland, but he doesn't naw what two an' three maks.'

'Five!' retorted George with a wink at Mark, 'pints o'bitter, in pint pots. Fill 'em up again, Mark.'

Betty called from the dining-room as we got our fill. The long oak table, clothless but highly polished, was laid out with side plates, cutlery, a huge jar of pickles and another of pickled red cabbage. Dave started off badly by knocking over the oak form he was to sit on, and in an effort to regain balance, sent his fork flying. Then Betty came in with the tray and the five plates, piled high with the tatie pot, and placed them before us. She was instantly accused of giving Dave the largest share, and the highest meat content. George made as if to slap her bottom as she went by but received a clipped ear for his trouble. Generous helpings of pickled onions and cabbage were ladled out, and we fell to as if we had not eaten for a week. We had hardly finished when Betty came in again and asked if we wanted seconds. She was greeted with a cheer and our plates were soon whisked away to return full.

'Watch it!' said Dave, pointing his fork at Billy. 'You can't get a quart into a pint pot.'

'I haven't filled a corner yet,' protested Billy, spooning out more pickles.

It was delicious and filling, and my consumption rate had declined by the time Betty again came in and said that there was more. There was a mixture of groans and cheers. Dave and George accepted more, generous helpings. The rest of us were content with a 'la'l spoonful'.

Hardly had we tucked this away before five plates of smoking apple pie were brought in, with a dish of cream, and a large pot of coffee. The pie pastry melted in my mouth and the apple was sweet and rich with juice. Half way through this ambrosia a huge cheese was dumped with a thump in the middle of the table; and another bowl, of biscuits, and a dish of white local-made butter. The conversation wilted under this new gas-tronomic onslaught but this was not the end of it. As we were hacking our way into the cheese Betty again came in, followed by Mark. She was carrying a cake, a modest-sized cake, lit with candles. There was a shout of approval. Billy looked surprised, and moved. Led by Mark's tuneful baritone we all sang 'happy birthday', and Billy had to blow out the candles and make the first cut. Stanley then horrified us by eating cheese with his cake. 'He's a Yorkshireman,' explained Dave. 'They've queer ways o'er yon.'

Although I would much rather have settled for a chair by the log fire by this time, we were instantly plunged into a game of darts, Mark joining in to make two teams of three. We lost count of time. Mark left us as the bar filled and Dave went to 'give a hand', ignoring the sly comments. Soon 'last orders' were being called and we finished our last hard-fought game.

We went out into a beautiful star-lit night, clear and cool. It was too fine to go home at once, and we leaned on Dave's van and talked. Somehow we got around to talking about pheasants. There were some, said Dave, as fat as geese, at oak coppice corner. He saw them feeding there nearly every day, and they roosted, he could swear, in those old yew trees by the side of the forest wall.

Stanley went on to say that if you knew where the beggars roosted you could shine a torch up the tree, beat it with sticks, and when the dazed birds dropped down you could just pick them up and wring them. Billy confirmed this and said that his 'grandfayder' had caught them that way. Somehow, it was such a splendid night, we decided to test the theory. It would not be poaching, we agreed, for the wood was 'ours'; and nobody, as far as we knew, had shooting rights there. The pheasants belonged, perhaps, to the neighbouring landowner. But who was to be sure of that? They had free run of the wood and could have bred there. In fact we occasionally took the odd bird. I caught one once which had got itself tangled in a wire netting tree enclosure.

So we all piled into the van. This time I sat in the back with a coil of rope, an axe, a billhook, a tool chest, and Stanley. The great starlit sky swirled around, and jerked to and fro, above our heads. Then great branches swept by, the heavier limbs pivoting the moving waves of twigs and leaves. Everyone was singing a hunting song and the wheezing, rattling exhaust pipe played an obbligato.

Presently we pulled up with a fierce jerk at the place where the road sweeps by the tarn. The alders and junipers stood out in jet black, irregular and crooked shapes in front of the flat calm shining level of the little lake cupped so perfectly in the fingers of the great wood beyond; the grey-black cloud-like hardwoods, spired with the black spires of spruce. We all got out, rubbed our sore places, and feasted our eyes on it. We had suddenly gone quieter. Dave passed round some small cigars while we discussed a plan of action. Dave, we decided, was far too noisy a character to take a leading part. We even, to his indignation, considered leaving him behind. But at last we settled that he would carry the large lantern that we fished out of his toolbox. George climbed over the wall with the bill-hook and presently returned with five stoutish cudgels. We looked a pretty desperate lot, more like bandits than hunters. We realized the absurdity of the situation when we received the weapons, and had a good laugh. But the die was cast. I am sure that we all had doubts about the outcome of the expedition but it was a fine night for a walk.

When the cigars were finished Stanley took the lead and we

went through the gate and along the track which led into the wood. Dave had strict instructions not to use the lantern, and as we approached the edge of the forest our eyes were getting accustomed to the starlight. Pipistrelle bats flicked out of the wood to meet us, perhaps to take the moths that we were stirring up from the grass. Certainly they are always there as you approach, flicking about, now above your head, now whisking by at shoulder height; in and out of the darkness like shadows in firelight. Somewhere on the mosses behind us a nightjar rattled.

We progressed fairly quietly in single file. If Stanley froze in his tracks we were all supposed to do the same; though in fact what happened was that four of us stopped dead and Dave collided with the rear of the column and swore, nullifying our efforts to observe without being observed. Once inside the wood we had to adjust our eyes again, then Stanley led us confidently to the boundary wall, which we began to follow towards oak coppice corner. We had not gone far alongside the wall when I heard a 'clump' behind me, an 'ouch!' from Billy, and then some confused noises. I turned to see nobody, then was dimly aware that there were struggling bodies on the ground. A branch had felled Billy, who in turn had demolished the rearguard. We had another conference. Billy pointed out that since we were following the boundary wall in any case we might as well follow it outside the wood where there was more light. He said he knew every inch of the ground outside the wood at this point, the field on the south side of the tarn, as he fished the tarn regularly. So we decided to climb the wall. No mean task, as it was quite high and in danger of collapse. We took it cautiously, one at a time. Dave swore heavily at the other side and said that he had torn the pocket of his coat. His best suit, too. The one he got for his brother's wedding five years ago, and he had kept it as good as new.

Having pacified Dave, we struck out boldly across the field, this time with Billy in the lead. The light was certainly better, and we could see the tarn, well to our right, very clearly. But the ground was tussocky and moist, and not at all easy to walk on. In fact the more we progressed the worse it became. It was almost like walking across a ploughed field. As each saw his preceding comrade stumble it was natural to seek another line of progress, so before long we were straggled out in a line abreast. If the walking was bad, everything else was perfect. The night was wonderful, the air was clean and cool and tinged with the smell of pines, moss, and moist earth. We felt full, and fit and heroic. Who would wish to lie abed on such a night! This was a night for adventure! We walked, and stumbled, picked ourselves up, and walked on gaily for some time, stifling George's inclination to burst into song.

Billy and I were at one end of the line. I saw him stop and look around. We had entered a hollow in rather darker shadow, and I noticed that there was no sign of the others. He looked at me, a puzzled expression on his long face. I looked around and back at him, equally baffled. Sometimes, when something extra-ordinary happens, all in a fraction of a second, time takes on another dimension. One is shocked into a much higher level of awareness. So, on this occasion, I experienced a strange impression of slow motion. In it I saw Billy's eyes and face change from surprise, to perplexity, and then, it seemed, very slowly to terror. The next thing I noticed was that, although Billy was a tall lad, his face was only on a level with my shoulder and was sinking lower. Then he was gone. At the same time I felt the ground shudder under my feet. 'My God!' I thought, 'This is a bog. Deep, deep mud, and we are all done for! They've all gone under and only me left!'

For what seemed minutes, but what must have been only fractions of a second, I experienced the extremities of panic. I felt the earth beneath me sinking rapidly, and then I was back-pedalling, scrambling for the firm land I had just left. Somehow I made it, sick with fear, and trembling all over. I looked around again but I could see none of my comrades. I was completely alone and in utter silence. I thought, 'My God! What can I do?'

Then, to my inexpressible relief, I heard a low mumbling, and curses, which could only mean that at least Dave was alive somewhere, even if he was in dire danger. To my amazement I then saw what appeared to be a head sticking out of the ground in front of me. I edged carefully towards it. Hands, and then arms, stretched out towards me. Extraordinary noises were coming from the head.

It was Billy's head. His mouth was open and his face was as stern as ever. His eyes were staring wide. I was considerably alarmed by the convulsive snorts, and gasps, and cackles coming from him. Then suddenly I realized with a shock that this was Billy laughing. Laughing as he had never laughed before. He was practically hysterical.

'Ho! Ho! Help us – Ho! Ho! Help us out!'

I leaned forward, grabbed his jacket collar and heaved. At the same time I noticed, stretching diagonally to my right, a long black slit in the ground.

Billy, still laughing like mad, and I walked along its edge and below we located the others, cursing and trying to get out. It was a gully about six feet deep, the end of a drainage channel which a former landowner had caused to be cut many years before to impound more water for his tarn. The sides had eroded and the top edges were crumbly. To say the least.

Luckly the bottom was dry and soft and we pulled everyone out. We lay on the grass and laughed, till a flock of wood-pigeons in a tarn-side oak could stand it no longer and clapped off into the darkness. We castigated Billy for saying he knew the area so well; then we debated whether to proceed or return. We reluctantly decided on the latter course, so we shall never know from experiment if the dazzle-pheasant-catching technique really works. George and Dave, for their part, swore that it could not. 'If it did,' said George, who was a great hunting man as well as a wrestler, 'every bloody fox in the country would have a lantern; and there wouldn't be a pheasant between Dunmail and the Bay.'

With no more mishaps except a few wet feet we arrived back at Dave's van. There was a roar when Dave said that he could not find his ignition key. We helped him to search, but without any luck. Dave pointed to his torn pocket. 'That's where the beggar is,' he said, 'by the wall where we climbed over.' He and

Stanley went back to search with the lantern while the rest of us sat around and talked. They were gone a long time and came back empty handed.

'It's really gone this time,' grumbled Dave. 'I'll have to search for it in daylight. May have dropped it in that drain.' We all groaned. We argued about the best way of starting the van without a key, but Dave said that nobody was going to mess about with the wiring. He had just fixed it after a lot of trouble. It was a lovely night and the walk home would do us all good. George picked Dave up and shook him. 'Ya gert addle-brain,' he grumbled.

'Come on, George,' said Stanley. 'It's safer to walk anyway.' We all agreed most readily.

So it was a case of walking a mile or more home. George had farthest to walk as he had come over the fell before meeting us at the crossroads, and he continued to mutter quite a lot about Dave's forgetful and clumsy habits. Billy, too, had to walk all the way back to the Punch Bowl for his motor-cycle. Eventually we reached the crossroads. Cigarettes were lit and we talked about work, and hunting, and women, and fishing, until the first flushes of the early summer dawn lightened the eastern fell. Then we dispersed our separate ways. I for one felt very tired, and as soon as I had fed Buck I intended hitting the sack.

I had not gone far along the road when I heard Dave panting behind me. 'Which is nearer,' he asked, 'your place, or my van?'

'Your van, I suppose,' I answered with some surprise.

'Come on back then,' he said. 'I'll give you a lift.'

'But the key – '

'Found it. In my cigarette case when I got a fag out. I remember I put it there for safe keeping.'

'But why didn't you tell the others?'

Dave gave me a quick look. There was an embarrassed silence.

'Well – ' he said at last with an uneasy grin, 'I thought it best to say nowt. No use asking for trouble is there?'

14 *Territories and Ways*

Most creatures are territorial – they have their little estate on which they live, and feed, and breed. They defend it very vigorously. They often mark off or declare their boundaries. In the case of birds they will shout – or sing – their heads off if an invader threatens to cross the invisible frontier. The stag roars his claim when he has assembled his wives. The fox marks with the scent of his own urine as do many of the carnivores. The roebuck is more specific. He marks by sight and scent. He 'frays' the young saplings on his frontier – scrapes the bark off with his growing antlers – and at the same time spreads his scent from a gland located at the base of the antlers. The mark is unmistakeable. One can see at once whether a woodland has roe deer in it or not.

The territorial instinct is self-protective. It ensures a constant food supply for the animal, and the family it intends to raise. It facilitates an even spread of the species. When a habitat is overcrowded there is trouble: hunger, fighting, and disease, and vulnerability to predators. In nature this kind of imbalance is unusual, and normally short-lived. It is only the human animal that has prolonged difficulties. The territorial instinct prompts the building of our walls; but our protective instincts extend to other territories – class, pride, or a set way of thinking. Basic animal instincts are at the seat of human emotions. We can hardly ever think or act without their influence. We cannot ignore them.

What we call 'nostalgia' is instinctive too. The pull of 'home' is quite basic. It pulls migratory birds thousands of miles across continents and oceans on clearly defined but invisible roads. For many creatures have two seasonal territories for feeding and breeding. Frogs head for their breeding pond as surely as if pulled by threads; and if a motorway is built across their path they will cross it in the early spring and get killed in hundreds. The red deer herds go off to their higher pastures in summer. Trout and salmon are pulled up their rivers at breeding time to battle against incredible currents and up fearsome falls. The regular ways are followed as if creatures carried maps in their brains. In the human animal the migration occurs at holiday times, and the roads they take, more often than not, follow the tracks that were made by the earliest humans.

A field naturalist, who has lived in one area for many years, knows where he has a good chance of seeing foxes, or badgers, or deer, or any named species of bird. He knows their ancient roads and their territories. Fox hunting in the Lake District is only possible by using this knowledge. Hunting has to be done on foot in the rough fell country and can be followed effectively only by watching the line the fox is taking; anticipating his next possible move from experience and making for the next vantage point. To the uninitiated it would seem that some of the older members of the hunt are almost clairvoyant. They know the ways of the local foxes, and yet are held by the fascination of the hunt because there is always the unusual individual which will confound anticipation, and choose a line which a crony will tell you in the bar afterwards 'was took by that girt dog fox that was lost at millbeck in that cold February in '56'.

When I was a boy I knew a gnarled hawthorn by the lake where a tawny owl liked to sit, and I could watch him, calling in the moonlight. Twenty-five years later I was passing the place at night, recognized the distinctive tree – and there was a tawny on the same perch. The peregrine falcons on a certain crag were shot by some sportsman one year. Ten years later, although there are scores of similar crags in that part of the district, a pair of peregrines chose the same nesting place: alas, to be persecuted again. The top stones – known by drystone wallers as 'cams' – on my garden wall are always being knocked down at the same point. For the wall was built across the ancient track of roe deer, and although it was made high, and on top of a high bank to boot, the roe jump and cross at this point. I know quite a few of these old roe tracks, where they cross the motor road between the wooded slopes and the rich feeding areas near the lake shore. Alas, some of the roe get killed by traffic in the night crossing. For if a roe has committed himself to cross the road, and sees the approaching lights of a fast-moving car, instinct tells him to run for it – an instinct which will get him out of most trouble, but is no help in motor traffic.

Late one night a knock came on my door and there stood a distressed young man asking me I could despatch a deer he had hit with his car. It was lying by the roadside badly injured. He had telephoned the police station and the constable on duty had told him to contact me as I was near the scene and better able to perform the duty. (I told the officer later that this really was 'passing the buck' – literally! Though in the event it was a doe.) I knew where the accident had happened without being told. It was a regular deer crossing place on the brow of a hill.

The adult doe was lying on the grass verge in the torch light, and kicking its back legs. Its back was broken. I avoided those legs, as many a hunter has been seriously hurt by a kick from a wounded roe. I took the knife, for I had no gun, and put my arm round its shoulder to lift up its head and neck. Its great eyes were already glazing. The warm hair in my fingers felt moist and lifeless. A dribble of bright red blood dripped from its partly open mouth. I hesitated before preparing to find the place to put the knife. It was providential. For in that moment I felt her go limp. She had died in my hands.

I laid the doe down gently. My feelings would be hard to explain. I certainly felt angry. Is it not enough that we shoot them needlessly? Or that we destroy and divide their habitats? To mangle them with our wretched steel boxes is too much.

After a moment I spoke to the young man, who was still there, holding his torch. I asked him if his car was all right.

'Badly damaged. Wing and headlight only though, I think. I can drive it.'

I vented my anger on him by saying that he must have been travelling some; and adding, with relish, that his car insurance would certainly provide no cover for damage by wild animals. Which was very unkind of me, I admitted to my conscience later, as the poor fellow had at least been concerned about the animal's suffering.

One Saturday night Dave and I were travelling back, from a very rare night out, in Dave's van. It was just after dusk. As we rounded a bend in the road near the approach to the Great Wood, Dave slammed on the brakes as his light picked out a body in the road. There was a motor-cycle upside down on the bank. To our horror the road was also splattered with blood. I jumped out and ran to the body, while Dave, with commendable imagination, reversed the van back a little down the road so that a car approaching the bend could see the rear lights. He kept his headlights on.

With hammering heart I examined the body then pulled it gently to the road side. It was Billy. He looked up at me, spat blood, and gasped, 'Is it John, then?' Which was rather an odd thing to say under the circumstances.

'Where are you hurt, lad?' I asked.

Billy moved both his arms, then lifted each leg in turn.

'I don't think I am. Just scraped and dented. How's the bike?'

'Never mind the bike for a moment,' I said. Billy's jacket was covered in blood. All over its front. But I could not find the source. His right trouser leg was practically torn off, and the skin scraped from the hip to the knee. But it was not bleeding badly at all. His lips were cut but his teeth intact.

Billy struggled to a sitting position and his stern face glowered at me.

'What'd'y'mean, never mind the bloody bike!'

'Let's worry about you first.'

'I'm all right, you damn fool.' He ran a fingerless glove over his bloody jacket. 'This mess must be roe guts!

It was only then that I noticed the very dead deer lying on the verge near the bike. Billy limped over, rubbing his head and moaning. He looked at the bike.

'Bent forks. Buckled wheel. Smashed light and speedo. Could have been worse.'

He then explained what happened. He had rounded the bend and had seen the roe on his right in the act of crossing. He slammed on the bike's brakes, but the deer jumped and he hit it with his headlamp, then tangled with the wall, and did a dive.

'I knew the beggar would bolt for it. But there was nowt I could do.'

I shone Dave's lantern to both sides of the road. In either walls there were the tell-tale missing cam stones. It was a regular deer route. In fact some years later there was a similar, almost carbon-copy, motor cycle and deer collision on the same spot.

But the incident had a strange ending. Out of the night came a sports car, which braked at the scene of the accident. A well-dressed gentleman with impressive moustache got out and asked, 'Anyone hurt?'

We assured him that all was well, and explained what had happened.

'Sorry if I make a cheeky request, old man,' he said, 'But do you mind if I take the deer? Partial to a bit of venison.'

So there it was. He wrapped the deer's body in a copy of *The Times*, popped it in his car boot and took it away. I felt just a little sick.

We heaved Billy's bike into the van and took him home. He had merely wrecked his suit and gloves and suffered bruises and scrapes.

When the Major, my employer, called in one evening to see how Buck was progressing, we got to discussing the movements and tracks of deer. The roe are great wanderers. This is another reason for their successful survival in Britain over thousands of years. If their habitat is overcrowded, or threatened, they will move over very long distances, and swim the rivers and lakes. And sometimes they will just move on, it would seem, for no real reason at all. I have seen a lone buck in a treeless area of Wasdale, grazing among sheep, no doubt on his way to seek a new woodland home. Red deer, on the other hand, are just a little more predictable. Like the roe, they are a woodland animal, but as the forest cover in the British Isles has decreased through the depredations of man and human settlement, they have adapted their ways and will live quite happily on the open moorlands. In such an area the roe would be very vulnerable, and in any case he is a browser rather than a grazer, much subject to attack from parasites if he grazes too long. The larger red deer is protected by its exceptionally keen eyesight, as well as its sense of smell. Its sentinels, usually elderly hinds, can see danger a long way off and the herd can be warned.

The red deer has not been settled in Britain all that long. It is assumed to have crossed the fordable North Sea from the continent a mere 400,000 years ago. It thrived. The great strong antlers of the woodland stag were used as pickaxes by the early settlers for hundreds of years, and venison was one of their main sources of food. Now few of the original herds are left in the British Isles. They exist only in the Lake District, and in Wales and Scotland. In other areas they were re-introduced after being killed off.

In the Lake District the best specimens of red deer are found in the heavily wooded areas of the Lancashire portion, and south Westmorland. The thriving Martindale herd in Westmorland does not have the same rich woodland diet as its southern and western neighbours. It roams the fells. Consequently it is a lighter animal, and the stags have less impressive heads as a rule.

The Major had shooting rights in the forest area on the far side of the lake; and one of his duties was to control the numbers of deer there. The word 'control' too often means 'kill off'. Massacres have been carried out in the name of 'control'. In this case, though, it meant that the deer were counted regularly, were frequently inspected, and the weakly animals, or poor stags carrying a 'bad head' – poorly-formed antlers which are often a sign of other physical deficiencies – were periodically shot. The Major offered to take me on one of his stalks, and I accepted.

It was another fine summer day when he called, with the promise of a clear evening. We drove down to a friend's boathouse on the lake shore, and picked out a dinghy. The Major explained that we would be returning in the early hours of the following morning and the ferry would not be running. Hence the need for our own boat.

So we put our rucksacks, and the Major's carefully-wrapped gun, in the boat, climbed in and pushed off. It was a long row, with the sun beating down on our backs and reflecting from the ripples. As we pulled I watched the slopes of Great Wood recede until it was all a dark and dappled mass on the far shore. When we beached I could just seen the point of Great Crag.

We pulled the boat well up, shouldered our burdens, and walked. We toiled up a slope into alders and hazels, then oaks, and on and up steeply into the plantations of spruce – sitka, which is in my opinion not an ugly tree, with its dark green foliage, shining grey underneath when rocked by the wind, but very nasty to walk through as its needles are horribly sharp, and the scratches irritate. Then up through larches, light-green and redolent; and older plantings of Norway spruce. As we neared the summit of the wood we sat down, ate a sandwich and opened our first flask, and the Major explained what we had to do. It was about four in the afternoon.

'I know where the herd is now,' he said. 'I know where it will feed at dusk, all things being equal. We're going now to a place which overlooks this area, and we're going to sit there without moving unduly, or making a single sound for a long time. The wind is just about right. If you make any sound from now on, or particularly later when we're in position; we might as well pack up and go home because the blighters will be off to feed elsewhere. So let's start and check. Have you any coins in your pockets?'

I told him I had.

'Break them up, put them in different pockets so they won't jingle together. Pull your hat well down and keep the brim over your eyes.' He gave me a piece of green cloth on a strand of elastic. 'Put that round your neck, and pull the cloth up to hide the white of your face when I tell you to. Beards are the best camouflage on a job like this. Did you bring gloves like I said? Good. They'll cover your white hands and keep the midges off your wrists when they start biting. They're killers up here. Now from now on, no talking unless it's absolutely necessary – sign language is better. Breathe the words if you have anything important to say. No sudden movements. Take it steady. Follow me, and for God's sake watch where you put your feet!'

We had not gone far when I was foolish enough to brush against a protruding dead twig which snapped off, with, it seemed in the silence, a noise like a clap of thunder. The Major turned round with a face distorted with acute anguish and reproach. I breathed an apology. We waited for some minutes so that any creature that might have heard us would be reassured, then we carried on up the slope.

The summit of the wooded fell was wide and undulating and broken by crags. This wood was broken by swampy areas and small tarns. The varied ground also meant a varied grouping of trees – coppice oak in the better drained area, with, surprisingly, some uncoppiced stands of very old sweet chestnut. Alders dominated the wetter areas, mixed with birch; which really came into their own on the rocky land. Amongst it all, as if grouped in battalions ready to assemble for battle, the plantations of larch and spruce. We were walking in zigzags over the very rough terrain, keeping to the cover of the trees, and moving roughly south west. The Major kept checking the wind, which was coming generally, very lightly, from the south east. We stopped under a holly tree for a rest. He took a twig and drew a stag's head on the soft ground. One of the antlers was thrust forward and lacked the normal tines.

'I only want that one,' he breathed. 'I've been trying for it for too long. Let's hope it turns up today. Now – dead silence!'

We walked for another fifteen minutes, slowly and carefully. In one very boggy area we had to stride softly from alder root to alder root. If we made the slightest sound, or if a bird started up in front of us, the drill was to keep still for several minutes. Jays are the worst things to rouse. Their raucous alarm cry is the early-warning system of the forest. Presently the Major indicated by signs that we had to cross the open area in front of us, to a hump of heathery crag, and that we had to keep down. He tested the wind in boy scout manner, by wetting a finger, and them moved off in a crouched position. I followed. The Major suddenly froze as if turned to stone. I did likewise and waited. In front of us was one crooked old oak. From it a buzzard lifted itself on great silent wings and spiralled upwards. We waited until it was out of sight before moving on.

We reached the crag with relief. The Major lay down and crawled up nearer the summit. This offered us a soft couch – and a supply of bilberries. He nodded at me and we relaxed. The sandwiches came out again. At the Major's suggestion we had

wrapped them in cloth, rather than noisy paper. We settled
down for a long wait. Sitting, fairly motionless, and in silence, is
tolerable for about half an hour. After that, for my part, I start
twitching and want to walk around, or clear my throat, or
whistle, or scratch. There was one anxious moment when the
buzzard returned and circled, decided that the things in the
heather might be suspicious, and moved off. Wait again. It
needs practice, this waiting. I peered into the heather and
watched a little red mite moving about there. An ant came and
picked up one of the bread crumbs. Then there were more and I
began to worry in case we were sitting on a nest of them.

A relief came when the Major's sharp ears eventually picked
up something, and with painful slowness he crawled with the
gun to the crag top. I pulled my cloth mask on and followed.
Very slowly the Major brought his head over the summit and
froze. So did I. Below us was a fine roebuck, grazing on the high
green grass of a long clearing. To my surprise the Major lifted
his rifle very slowly, and took aim. I need not have worried. He
was merely using his telescopic gun-sight to examine the beast.
We crawled slowly back again and he grinned at me. Then the
long silence once more.

As the evening approached the midges came. It was torture.
We were pinned down, motionless, and could offer no resistance. Word got around among the whole midge population of
the wood that we were helpless and tasty and they queued up in
clouds to make their landings. I recalled the stories of savages
pegging victims to earth, and allowing them to be slowly devoured by ants. I fastened my shirt collar and turned it up;
pulled my hat as far down as it would go. I took a keen interest
in the bilberry plants. The tiny delicate leaves. I pulled them off
and ate them. Leaves, flowers and berries of bilberry. I tasted
them all. They all have the same, sharp acidity which is quite
pleasant to me. The Major, too, was not too happy about the
midge attacks. But he was giving them the stiff upper lip treatment. The long day stretched out, and the dusk seemed as far
away as ever.

At long last the Major put up a cautionary hand, and began

the slow crawl up to the summit again. I followed. What I saw was a surprise. The glade seemed full of moving, grazing red deer. They were so near I could have hit them with a stone. I never expected to get so close. There were twelve hinds, and three young stags. I could make out two young calves following in the long grass, and there must have been others lying in the area. But no adult stags for some time. Then, disdainfully apart from the females, came an adult stag, with the makings of a very fine head of antlers, beautifully arched and sturdy with ten points. There were more deer only dimly sighted in the distant end of the glade. We watched and waited. The major looked along his gun-sight at the good stag, and turned his head to me to grin his approval. As time went on there were less deer to be seen, the light was worsening. The Major was now using binoculars to search the end of the clearing and he was looking unhappy. The stag he wanted was not in sight, After, I suppose, about an hour or more, he gave up. We crawled back down the crag, the rifle was recovered, and we retreated across the swamp.

I cannot say that I was disappointed. But the Major was very depressed. He now walked quickly and quietly and I had a job to keep up. I appreciated why he was in a hurry, for the light was going, and when it is dark in the open, it can be as black as the eighth plague of Egypt in unfamiliar woodland. This time we headed south, wading at times through swamp and water, until we eventually found an old timber trail which left the summit plateau and began to descend to the lake. Here the Major relaxed and talked normally. We stopped and opened another flask.

'Well,' he said, 'I'd hoped to get him tonight but he's taken himself off. Better luck next time. I must get him before the rut. What did you think of that fine one? I've watched him coming on. Man, he's a beauty!'

It was quite late and very quiet when we reached the cottage at the end of the timber trail and some distance from the shore. A beck tumbled past it, and an old motionless mill wheel. The Major took out a notebook, scribbled a note, and pushed it through the cottage's letter box. 'Just to tell Tommy I'll not need to borrow his tractor to bring in the carcase – this time!'

We struck down to the lake and followed a path along its edge. The water was flat calm and utterly silent. There is hardly anything more impressive than a great sheet of water which is motionless and soundless. At such rare moments at sea it is almost frightening.

Much to my surprise, for I was completely lost now and stumbling behind the Major in the dark, we were suddenly at our boat. We loaded, and pushed off. It was hardly possible to see the level of the water to dip in the oars.

'Row right across and we'll recognize landmarks on the other side,' I was told. 'The moon should be up a bit by the time we get there.'

It was a very odd sensation, rowing through the dark. But for the sound of the oars rippling the water, and the bow ripple, we might have been airborne. But as we got well out there was a lightening in the sky. The moon was coming; and not far in front of the dawn. As we went on slowly the tip of it edged over the fell and a line of silver marked the lake. It was only the tip of a thin slice of moon but it was enough. When we reached the far side the Major pointed out a jetty he knew and we struck down the lake. The whole shore was brooding in silence. A grey boathouse, a moored yacht, a tree-crowned promontory, then a line of boats tied to a 'trot' mooring, a jetty and a solitary light shining from an hotel window. Bats swooped around us at one point, skimming the lake surface as the swallows had done in the daylight, hours before. There was a plop as a heavy fish took to air, and the Major said that he had a good mind to get out his rod when we got back. More boathouses and a jetty later, we were turning towards our starting point. We beached and I looked back.

Now the lake was truly a shining level. It was silvered and the surface blinked in a slight ripple. We looked at it, as the Major lit his pipe, and let the shimmering beauty of it soak in. We looked at it for long moments, then the Major said, 'Come on!'

He drove me back and dropped me at the gate.

'I'm off back,' he said, 'for my rod. I'll get me a fish for breakfast at least.'

I watched the rear lights down the road and walked to the hut. It was getting lighter now. As I reached for the door handle I heard a movement behind me. Buck was there, a few feet away. His head was erect, ears forward, eyes bright. He crowded into the hut with me, and watched as I lit the gas mantle.

15 Return to Solitude

As the summer progresses, more and more people give way to
their migratory instincts to re-create themselves; at the sea, the
source of life; or in the countryside where it is more apparent
and accessible. They come to the Lake District in thousands.
Those who seek to get away from it all; and those who bring it
all with them. Those who seek peace and solitude; and those
who want lots of congenial company. Those who lift up their
eyes unto the hills; and those who lift up their hiking boots to
them. The Lake District absorbs them all. On the busiest day of

a Bank Holiday, even the solitude seeker, if he is prepared to walk, can find his desire.

The lane past my hut was getting busier. The camp and caravan sites a mile away were showing signs of life. And more people were knocking at my door and asking to see Buck. I like people, provided that there are not too many around at once. Buck did not like them particularly. They were noisy. They moved about too much; and tried to touch him. They offered him inedible objects and disturbed him in his afternoon nap. Two other considerations persuaded me to think of returning to my secluded shelter: the need to do some maintenance work on that side of the wood; and the necessity to have some peace and quiet to meet my writing commitments.

So I planned to leave the hut, of which I had now grown very fond. It welcomed me every time I came to it; not the welcome of a well-known and well-loved friend, but the kindly, reserved welcome of a wise patriarch. It had affected me, perhaps. Dave put it more directly as he looked round the walls and then at me one evening: 'You look more foxy every time I see you. And when you get worked up you snarl just like that beggar in the corner.' I still remember every detail of that room with affection. The smell of wood smoke, catching me unawares, often reminds me of it.

But I wanted to continue my desert island existence now it was high summer. I wondered if Buck would take to it, or whether he now considered the hut his personal territory.

I transferred my few necessities as before, but I also took a pick and shovel, an iron rake and a wheelbarrow, as I was going to clear some old drains and culverts in that end of the wood to maintain an old extraction road.

I started off with the wheelbarrow, with Buck, as usual, browsing his way behind me. Half way to our destination it started to rain. It really can rain in the Lake District. The rain clouds drift in from the Atlantic, open up on the mountains, and fill the lakes. Sometimes, after days of heavy rain, when the lake levels rise, we wonder if we are going to finish up with just one large lake instead of the sixteen. Unfortunately, heavy rains often coincide with the height of the holiday season, and many of those who endure it vow that they will go abroad on the following year, and risk sunstroke. One has two choices. If you are fit and vigorous, and your holiday accommodation has lots of drying facilities, you go out and get wet. For so long as you keep warm, wetness is not harmful. Layers of woolly clothing retain heat even if wet, so long as one is not enduring the strong winds that come with the rain on the fell tops. Wet, windy conditions on the fells are highly dangerous. Many holidaymakers have died from exposure in mid-summer. The other alternative is to dress oneself from head to foot in waterproof gear, then go out and gently perspire all day. I used to make the former choice. But after taking part in one terrible July mountain rescue, when several of the team members had to return to the valley suffering from the first stages of exposure from the wind and wetness, I, and other members of the mountain rescue team, bought waterproof suits. I now regard mine as one of my most precious possessions.

But on this occasion I was in the wool-and-face-it category. As soon as I got to the shelter I gathered some needle-thin dead birch twigs and a great pile of other kindling and built a large fire. I gathered so much dead wood that the fire burned on even in the rain. Buck chose a spot on a bank overlooking the shelter and settled down to rest. Occasionally he stood up, puffed out the hair on his body, and shook himself like a large dog. Then he settled down again in the rain to his cud-chewing. I set a can of water near the fire, then went off with the rake to clear some gullies.

There is a fascination about messing about with water. It is quite basic. Children openly enjoy it. Adults take a more furtive pleasure in it. Clearing gullies, I told myself, was terribly important work. If it was not done the road surface would become eroded. So I started at the bottom, raked out the mess of leaves and mud and roots until a thin trickle of water appeared on the now clean soil. Then I worked up the slope, repeating the effort all the way along until the thin trickle became a small streamlet, then a tumbling, active stream; and then, the great joy! I had saved a dam of rubbish behind which had collected a deep pond near a steep drop. It lurked there, dark and still, waiting for the release of the savagery that was hidden in its depths. One flourish of the rake and it was off and away like a mad thing, pelting down the hillside and throwing any debris in its way contemptuously aside. It went down like a tidal wave, and if I had not been a dignified adult, but a young lad again, I would have thrown up my hat and run after it, and shouted, 'Hooray!'

Further on I found that the track surface was flooded. I traced the fault to another gully, filled with a pile of brash left by forestry contractors; springy larch branches that lay coiled, waiting. As soon as I released them with the rake they sprang up and showered me with mud. Then there were the tight-packed ones to deal with, interlocked masses that were the devil to move at all. Again I started at the bottom of the trouble, and worked my way back to the flood, raking the rubbish well away. Then again the release of the last dam, and the satisfaction of seeing the flood pour away to reveal the hard surface of the track.

I followed the track down to the bridge where all the springs eventually merge in one large beck before descending in a roaring cascade to the levels of the tarn. It was quite a sight.

On the way back I gathered some late cowslip flowers. Buck was still waiting in the same position on the bank near the shelter. I put the can of water closer to the heart of the fire, then stripped the cowslip flowers from the stalk. As soon as the water began to boil I took it off the fire and threw in the flowers, and let it brew. In Britain our favourite beverage is made from an infusion of dried leaves from a camellia which grows in the east. To its comforting fragrance we outrageously add the vulgar flavour of a substance made from the sap of a sub-tropical reed; and further insult it with a neutralizing fluid from the mammary glands of a domestic herbivore. Tea should be treated better. It should be strong and unmilked. A thin slice of lemon may be added, or a little mild honey if one has a sweet tooth. And, in cold weather, just the tiniest suggestion of whisky.

But in theory anyway one need not be hooked on tea. Are there not plants enough in Britain? On the continent one can drink a ptisan (what a good word for the crossword-puzzle setters!). A favourite ptisan is made from the flowers of the lime tree. It is invigorating and has a subtle flavour to anyone whose taste buds have not been ruined by nicotine. A comparable all-British ptisan can be made from elder flowers. Out of season, dried flowers are permissible. Camomile flowers are very fine, too. But cowslip has a good country flavour. In the old times cowslip tea was taken for sleeplessness, for it soothes the jaded nerves. That day there was nothing much wrong with my nerves. I just wanted to enjoy the flavour of it.

To me the sight, smell and feel of the countryside is not enough. I have to taste it! Friends who walk with me sometimes think I am quite mad. I have a habit of nipping off young leaf buds from trees to chew. This used to be a common practice of country people. The young buds of hawthorn, for instance, are still known in some places as 'bread-and-cheese'. There is a nice sharp tang, and a pleasant crispiness about young leaf growth. New grass stems, pulled out of their leafshield, are also delicious. The new shoots of larch, like miniature green shaving brushes, have a pleasing sharp acid taste. New heather tips are almost as good. Thin green birch twiglets are quite edible. Ash sap I can suck with pleasure from new-cut wood. Ash sap in old Scandinavia was revered as the blood of the tree of life: a nectar indeed. Birch sap is also refreshing, and was once the main ingredient of birch beer. Washing in birch sap, by the way, used to be an old beauty recipe; it was also said that the sap dissolves pearls! If one had the patience to draw sap from a sycamore, and boil it, the result would be a good syrup – the sugar maple is a relative. The resin, set hard on the side of wounds on conifer trunks, I also pick off and chew. It is a good chewing-gum, and one could chew it all day if one wished. Tiny young holly leaves, fresh green and not yet prickly, also provide a morsel of flavour. I have mentioned that they make a tolerable tea. In fact I have a go at almost every tree – except ivy. Ivy is a thing of beauty; the enormous variety of pleasing shapes, colours and veining of leaves, on the one plant, can give some moments of idle pleasure to anyone who has time to stop and stare; but its taste is very nasty.

I have not yet been poisoned. Some of my friends say that this is a miracle. But I believe that poisonous stuff has a warning look about it. I have never, for instance, had the slightest temptation to chew the glossy leaves of the cuckoo-pint, the arum lily. It is difficult to say why. I had been chewing up the countryside a long time before I knew that the stuff would blister your mouth if you tried it. Wild flowers and ground plants I have always treated with care, though violets are quite edible, and can be made into a sweetmeat, and rose buds are good. When I was a very small child I was punished for eating a handful of them – off a neighbour's bush. Buttercups are nasty, but daisies are fairly pleasant. I would never taste anything that has not a pleasing smell. Sorrel was Buck's favourite food, and I acquired a taste for its acidity, too, after a while. Wood sorrel has a similar tang. Lady's-smock is distantly related to cress and the leaves have a pleasant, peppery flavour. Tansy leaves taste of ginger and were once used in the country to make 'tansy pudding'.

Perhaps I obtained a desire to taste wild herbs when I was a young lad. In the bad times of the depression I was an ailing, worrying problem to my mother. I caught everything that came my way. Mother was told by someone to make me drink a herb concoction regularly. It came from the herbalist looking like dried lawn cuttings. When it was boiling the house was full of a strange, indefinable smell reminiscent of new-mown cricket-pitches, the wind on the heath, and old witches' cauldrons. Its taste at first was abominable. But after a while I acquired a liking for the evil-looking liquid. I can still taste it in memory. There are fewer herbalists' shops nowadays. For a few pennies in my youth I could go into one and buy a glass of cool black sarsaparilla; or dandelion and burdock; or a 'blood tonic' which tasted like a mixture of the two. Such delights are rarer now. Soft-drink manufacturers, with their artificial flavourings and colourings, and gas bubbles, and saccharine, produce nothing like those rich black concoctions that delighted our palates, and I am sure did us a world of good.

The rain had a somewhat damping effect on my culinary ambitions for the evening. I pushed eggs and potatoes into the embers, made some dough, twisted it round a stick, and put it very close to bake. I made extra twists to keep for later. After I had eaten my meal I stoked the fire up really high until the sod roof at the front of my shelter began to steam and then I sat in its entrance and enjoyed the heat. Buck by this time had vanished. This worried me a bit, though I reasoned that he knew where I was and was bound to return. But as the evening drew on there was still no sign of him. So I took another walk round with the rake, calling as I went.

I returned eventually, deer-less. I was thoroughly wet and I thought it was time I changed into something dry. I gathered up plenty of fuel again, and stacked it by the hut. I stirred up the fire until it was a roaring monster then stripped off my clothing and hung it on hazel rods I had driven into the ground beside it. It was while I was busy at this, and half-naked, that I was very startled by a movement at my side. Buck had returned, and he would like his warm milk now, if you please.

The rain had stopped by the morning, but I had slept too heavily. I had intended to wake up in the night to stoke the fire and turn the drying clothing. Now the fire was almost out and the clothing still wet. As I left my shelter to attend to this situation, the midges moved in. The midges of the Great Wood were a force to be reckoned with. They lacked the numbers that one finds in the highlands of Scotland, perhaps, or worse still on the arctic fringes of Scandinavia; but what they lacked numerically they made up for in ferocity and persistence.

'Midges?' Dave had remarked once. 'Those in Great Wood are as big as finches. They tear lumps off you and fly into the tree branches to eat them.'

Flies are also a nuisance in the woodland clearings. As if midges are not enough the muscids move in – irritating relations of the house fly that feed on sweat. They swarm in clouds around your head, landing on ears, and nose, and eyelids. The worst thing one can do is to lose one's temper. For this induces perspiration, which attracts more flies, which encourages more loss of temper and more perspiration until one is covered with flies and driven half mad. Then there are the clegs. These pussy-footed little horrors land undetected on bare limbs, and bite hard. They are creatures of wet places, mostly. I recall one terrible hot day when I was walking through a moorland swamp in shorts. By the time I had reached dry land my bare knees were literally running with blood. Animals suffer terribly from flies, and deer are no exception. Buck's sensitive ears were constantly flicking. It is often this sort of movement which helps the stalker to locate the deer in the summer.

Somewhere in the great pattern of nature flies have their place. But one cannot help feeling that that place is not one's eyes and ears. I look with gratitude to the insect eaters among the birds. Particularly the swallows and martins that beat about the wet places, gorging on them. And the dragonflies – surely the inspiration for the first helicopter designers – that hover and dart around the ponds, banqueting on flies. And the frogs and toads, and the evening-flying bats. Welcome friends!

After Buck and I had had breakfast I sat back and enjoyed the sunshine which had begun to shaft into the clearing. I allowed the soothing solitude to creep in on me.

Solitude is a glade close-pressed by trees – great thick clouds of trees, leaf-rippled by the warm air. It is the hum of summer insects; the slow pendulum swing of a silk-held caterpillar; the beckoning of a fern frond. And a deer in the dappled green shadows, eyes half closed, and jaws moving at the cud; ears turning to catch the hushed whispers of warning from the wood. True solitude is not loneliness. It is a great one-ness. One with everything: the cool grass, the deer, the glade, the wood, the countryside; this thin envelope of gas which gives our world life; the planet, the galaxy, the universe. It is not a loss; but a gift of wholeness. A wholeness with everything; body, spirit, mind, and the whole level of attention. A wholeness in the one moment of time poised in eternity.

I savoured it; and the warm comfort of it followed me as I

went to pick up my tools, and as I trundled the barrow down the steaming track. And it was not a track but the nave of a great cathedral, and the bird choirs are singing and –

And the damnable sacrilegious wheelbarrow spindle moaned, 'Oil me! – Oil me!'

16 Bug Hunts

On fine evenings, after a sunset which held no threat of rain, I would take my blanket and sleep out – anywhere so long as it was within reach of the shelter in case my weather forecasting was at fault. A favourite spot was on the highest place on my 'island' where the flies were not so bothersome. There was an outcrop of rock here with a shallow step in it, carpeted deep with larch and pine needles. I laid a heavy log on the open side of the step so that I had a comfortable little hollow. I would lie, on a clear night, looking upwards at the stars, and at that strange level of consciousness between waking and sleeping I might sometimes imagine that I was floating upwards and among them. If the wind freshened and rippled the treetops the sound was like breakers on the seashore. The coming of the night was always heralded by the woodcock. I could hear its soft 'croak-croak' followed by a high-pitched squeak. And the silhouette of this creature of the twilight would come between me and the sky as it made its way with quick, silent wing-beats to its feeding ground by the lake shore. Then, often, would come that strange whirr from the nightjar on the distant mosses.

Sometimes in the middle of the night I would be awakened by a slight sound and find that Buck had scraped away a bed nearby and honoured me with his company. This is an odd habit of the roe. Before they lie down for a nap they must scrape and scrape away until there is a bare patch to settle in. These bare patches are another tell-tale sign that there are roe in the woods.

On a still night it was possible to read by the light of a candle in a jam jar. But this often meant that I would be distracted by the suicidal swoops on the light from insects of all types; some of them rather horrific. The big moths were really disturbing.

I never took a great interest in moths until one day the Major told me that he was making a collection of the lepidoptera in the area and would appreciate my help. I shall always remember one of the first hunts. The Major was ill at the time, and I was visiting him in the early evening.

'It's a fine night for bug hunting,' he said. 'Mild, with just about the right humidity.'

I offered to take a net and a few of the glass-fronted pill boxes that he kept in an angler's satchel.

'Take these,' he said, offering me a large white sheet, and a powerful hand lamp. 'Put the sheet under a bush and spread it out. Fix the lamp up on a branch so that it shines on to the sheet. Then thrash the bush with a stick. Pick up the moths that land on the sheet.'

This sounded a crazy plan but I was willing to try. I found a good bush by the roadside. I did as I was told, and rigged up the sheet and lamp. When I hit the bush with a stick I was amazed to find that moths were falling like snow on to the sheet. They were so stupefied by the dazzle that it was very easy to scoop them into a pill box. The net was not necessary. So successful was I, that I had moths packed in two or three or more to a box. Glowing with excitement and satisfaction at my success I took my catch to the Major, who was sitting up in bed waiting. I spread the boxes on his eiderdown.

'Didn't take you long!' he remarked. 'Let's have a look.'

He picked up one box at a time and peered in through the window. He put some boxes on one side, glass side down, and some on the other. While he was doing this I noticed that not only had I filled the pill boxes, but my jacket was crawling with moths. They were coming out of folds, and pocket-flaps, and my lapels, and flying up towards the room light and the bedside lamp. The Major would look up from his boxes and point and say 'Net that one!' I would catch it and box it and add it to the pile he was studying.

Presently he packed a pile of boxes back into the satchel. 'Take these out, well away, and let them loose. Then come back and help me get some of these into the killing bottle.'

The first job was soon done; the second was harder. It was difficult to sort out the wanted ones in the boxes from the un-wanted, and we had to pack nearly all of them into the killing bottle, then fish out the latter and get rid of them. While this was happening, more moths that I had originally brought in in folds of my clothing, and which had dropped behind furniture and curtains, were emerging and flying round the light. Occasionally I had to jump up and net one. It was an exciting few hours, and the Major told me later that he was awake all that night pinning out his prizes. I do not think his doctor would have approved.

On odd evenings after this, and indeed on many days, for not all moths are night flyers by any means, I would take an hour or two off and go out with the net. I had some exciting hunts. What astonished me was the fantastic range of species to be found. I was very much against the idea of catching and killing moths until I found that there is really no other way of seeing these colourful creatures. Some of my favourites, though, were day flyers. The Cinnabar is a beauty, with its bright red wings with black-velvet markings. I took my first catch of these to the Major in triumph. This was surely a find! But all that glisters, in lepidoptera, as in other spheres, is not gold.

'It's one of the commonest moths,' he said. And sure enough it is. For the common ragwort is the food plant of the endearing caterpillars of this species – all striped, as if they are wearing football jerseys, and living in teams.

The very drab chimney sweeper moth is another favourite. They fly up in numbers as you disturb the ground foliage on a hot summer day, like tiny black bats.

Most people are completely ignorant about moths, think them rather nasty, and kill them on sight. They have perhaps a vague idea that they are pests. They eat clothing! In fact only the larva of one species, a quite tiny moth, is responsible for damage to clothing (though it has not yet found a taste for man-made fibres). It is something of a mysterious creature, which in its wild state probably lives very dangerously on the woolly linings of some birds' nests. But there are well over two thousand species of moth in the British Isles, all of them living on vegetation. Many of them live in our towns and suburbs, their larvae existing on their own particular food plant – mainly trees and weeds and, to a lesser extent, on the exotics of the gardens. I have known gardeners kill caterpillars on their trees, and even on roadside weeds nearby, in the mistaken belief that they will 'get on to the flowers and vegetables'. In fact, generally, each species can only feed on the particular food plants to which nature has allocated it. If one was to take the great fat green caterpillar with the pretty white stripes, the privet hawk, off the hedge, and try to feed it on any of the garden plants, with the exception of lilac, which is a close relative of the privet, the creature would die of starvation. Moth caterpillars offer no threat to the ordinary gardener. They rarely reach plague proportions, though fruit growers can have trouble with one or two species, such as the tiny codling moth, the winter moth,

March moth, and mottled umber. Those nasty colonies of voracious larvae that gardeners often find on gooseberry bushes are not moth caterpillars at all – they belong to one of the sawfly species. One good way in which gardeners can ensure freedom from plagues of insects of all types, is to encourage wild birds to nest by placing nest boxes. This is better, and cheaper, than the laborious and possibly dangerous use of chemicals.

Some of the moths are quite large and fat, like the privet and poplar hawk moths that fly around town gardens. In Lancashire big moths are known as 'night buzzerts' for some strange reason; and I remember being told as a boy that if one came into the house there would be a death in the family. It is sad that one can usually only see the full beauty of moths when they are killed, and their wings pinned to a board. Then that dull greyish creature which you netted reveals itself as an intricately patterned masterpiece. The so-called 'carpets', for instance, look drab in flight, but close examination in the light reveals their beautiful and elaborate markings that reminded early moth-hunters of the designs on eastern carpets. Those early entomologists, who gave us the English names, were certainly carried away with admiration for their finds. For a few examples of their naming: beautiful brocade; chinese character; crimson-speckled footman; the emperor; green-brindled crescent; tree-lichen beauty; elephant hawk; tiger; leopard; fox; argent and sable; brussels lace; ermine; burnished brass; emerald; maiden's blush. Not a lot of them are as gaudy as their butterfly cousins, but if they all flew, like them, in daylight, their beauty would be wondered at, and poets would have sung their praises. But they are known only to the entomologists.

One obvious way in which the Major collected his specimens was by a light trap. He set a powerful lamp by an open window, and on a good night they would home in on the light by scores. But not all moths are attracted to light; and one startling method of catching males was to cage a female moth, set it up on a wall or a tree stump, and wait. We caught the large northern eggar by this method, in daylight. The northern eggar is common in the Lake District and Scotland, and in the autumn the huge hairy caterpillars can sometimes be found in numbers feeding on the heather; not in colonies like some caterpillars, for the female lays her eggs in flight – bombing the vegetation as she goes. The males zoomed into the clearing, where we had set our female lure, at terrific speed. Entomologists say that the females are located by scent. This seems incredible to me. The males travel up-wind and must come from some considerable distance. The secret of their sensitivity is in their antennae, which vary in shape according to species, but generally have lateral hairs, sometimes looking like tiny feathers. They have the appearance, to me, of tiny high-frequency radio aerials. They must certainly be very finely tuned to receive the scent-waves of their females. Sometimes one might have difficulty in distinguishing butterflies from day-flying moths. The antennae check can show the difference. Our butterflies have 'clubbed' antennae – they end in a tiny knob.

It was one of these daylight moth hunts that nearly cut me down in my prime. The Major was keen on getting fox moths. These fly fast, and are consequently difficult to net. I climbed up through the heather of the nearby moor on a likely day. It was warm, and the peat dust rose as I walked. The summit was broken by crags, and the views west and north across the lake, which was some eight hundred feet below, were marvellous. I was sitting down to admire it all when I saw a light-brown moth zig-zagging rapidly in my direction. I got the net at the ready, then ran to intercept. It came right at me, too close to swing at, and I heard the hum of its wings as it swept past my face. I ran after it. Several times I got close enough to swing my net, but it evaded the trap by a hair's-breadth each time and kept on going. It then gained altitude a little and went off in a straight line. Nothing infuriates the hunter, whether of tigers or bugs, more than the tempting quarry that has been within reach, but just, and only just, and keeps getting away. The hunter is possessed by a reckless madness. Like a stoat, he is completely unaware of his surroundings. He can only see the quarry. In such a state was I, and I took off after that moth as if my feet had wings.

The moth was just above eye level and travelling fast. So I was running with my head up, stumbling like mad over the uneven ground and then – I ran right over the edge of a crag outcrop.

It took just one small moment from take-off to landing, but in it I was aware that my fall had become a dive, and strangely, or rather perhaps miraculously, I remembered somebody's advice – maybe my judo instructor, or one of my climbing companions? Anyhow, something reminded me to relax my body, take the fall on the shoulder, and allow myself to roll. And that is what I think I did. But I hit the ground so hard that the breath was knocked out of me. For a split second I wondered what I had broken, then I was rolling, very fast indeed, down a steep heathery slope, bouncing now and again over exposed boulders, When I eventually stopped I picked myself up very slowly, testing each limb. My shoulder and neck hurt abominably, but there were no breakages. I tasted blood, and discovered that I had done no worse than bite the edge of my tongue. I looked back at the crag. I suppose I had dropped about twenty feet, almost vertically, then bounced and rolled about a hundred. Several things contributed to save me from worse injury. It was not a dead-fall, but I had run right off the crag like the shell from a cannon, and it was more a kind of ricochet! The heather on the slope acted as an effective brake. At first I was mad. Really mad. Because that fox moth had got away, and was no doubt having fun with some vixen moths. Then I looked at my broken net and saw the humour of the situation and laughed like a crazy woodpecker. 'A hundred and twenty feet in one bound!' I said aloud. 'Man, you've got the world record!' And I laughed even more insanely at my feeble wit.

It was not long before I had a strange companion on my moth-hunting trips; none other than the massive George. It all started when George noticed, when he was manhandling some fence posts, that there was something odd on the nearby pile of bark that had been stripped off the posts. He went over to look and found a large-bodied moth that we later identified as a buff tip. It was clever of it to select the bark pile to rest on as it was perfect camouflage, and it was its movement that had attracted

George. George packed it into his cap and took it to the Major, who congratulated him on not doing it any damage. Pleased with his find, George then began to notice moths everywhere, and his strong hunting instincts were aroused. He did not come from the John Peel country for nothing. He found moths resting on tree trucks and ground vegetation, and developed a sharp eye for them.

In fact, moth hunting is not all netting, and often the best specimens are found at their roost. But George wanted to try his skill with the net.

'Next time tha gets out netting, just tell me,' he said to me, 'and I'll have a do with tha.'

So, a bit self-conscious at first, but later spurred on by his success, George took to bug hunting in earnest. One night the Major asked us if we would like to try a new method.

'We'll try owt,' said George.

The Major gave us a substance in two screw-top jars, and two wooden spatulas. 'Go along the lane,' he said, 'and spread this stuff on the tree trunks, a patch every ten yards or so. Leave it for an hour or more then take your lamp and pill boxes and pick off the moths feeding from it.' He explained that it was a mixture of demerara sugar, a drop of ale, treacle, and a good lacing of rum.

'It's a system often used by entomologists, though I've never tried it myself before,' he said. 'The moths are attracted by it. Can't resist it. They feed themselves stupid and you can pick them off with ease.'

It sounded crazy, but we agreed to try it. As soon as we had left the Major's, though, George seemed to have doubts. 'Are you sure the old fella's not going potty?' he said. 'Sounds sort o' far-fetched.'

'He's always been right so far,' I said.

George thought for a while then said, 'Tell you what. We'll dab this stuff on't trees along to t'lane to t'White Horse. Spend an hour or so there. And if the la'l boogars tak to the stuff, we'll pick 'em off on t'way back.'

I agreed to this plan and we set off. When we reached the first tree, George pulled the lid off his jar, and said, 'By gow, lad, this smells about ten 'orse power!' He dipped in his spatula and tasted it. 'And it tastes better than t'best Cumberland rum-butter!'

I didn't believe it, so had to try it myself.

'Tha'rt reet!' I agreed. So as we went along we dabbed a tree in the correct manner, and then, occasionally, dabbed our tongues. We marked a lot of trees, and by the time we reached the White Horse, we were feeling a warm glow inside.

'By gow!' exclaimed George. 'This stuff gives me a fancy for a taste o' rum. It reminds me of me old mum's rum-butter. Dammit, I'll even buy you one.'

As an ex-navy man I found it difficult to refuse.

So we went in, put our jars on a corner table, and had a couple of glasses. There was a bit of fun with the local lads, who wanted to know what was in our jars. George explained that it was linament, special stuff, as we were in training for the Grasmere Sports. But he told Elsie, the barmaid, that it was love potion. And if he was to give her one sniff of it, she would find him irresistible. She told him that it would have to be strong stuff indeed, to make George seem irresistible. We left at closing time, picked up our nets from the hazel clump outside, where we had left them, then we went cheerfully back to see what we had caught.

The first score of trees yielded nothing exciting. But as we were getting nearer home we began picking moths off in greater numbers. We hardly needed the nets. Most of them just fell into our pill boxes. We took particular care to pick up the drab looking ones. For these, George explained, in his experience, were the rare ones usually. 'And when he pins 'em out,' he said, 'they look like jewels. Look at 'em, lad. Fallin' into t'boxes. Droonk as lords! What a way t' go!'

Half-way back we stopped for a breather, and to my surprise George pulled a small bottle of rum out of his pocket. Then, as we progressed again, George started singing hunting songs, and grumbled at me for not holding the pill boxes still when he was trying to persuade moths into them.

I shall never forget the look of surprise on the face of the little man we found further down the lane. His car had had a puncture, and in the process of changing a wheel it had slipped off the jack and he could not get the jack out. To be suddenly confronted, at that late hour, by two strange men, one a singing giant, both carrying nets and haversacks and lanterns, must have made his blood run cold.

'Catch ho'd,' said George to me, grabbing a corner of the car. Together we lifted it. 'Now pull t'jack out!' he said.

The bemused motorist did as he suggested, and while we, or rather mostly George, held the weight, he replaced the jack, and we had the wheel changed in two minutes.

We quietened down when we neared the cottage where the Major lived. I pointed out to George that we would have to smarten ourselves up, or the man would think we had consumed all the contents of the jars ourselves!

'Dammit, aye,' said George. 'An' our breath'll smell o' rum too.' He dived his hand into a pocket and produced some sticky-looking objects covered in pocket-fluff. ' 'Ere. Let's suck a peppermint apiece. That'll put the auld hound off th'scent.'

What the Major thought, as we delivered the pill boxes of moths, I shall never know. But he told us, a few days later, that one of our catches was a rare one.

'By gow,' said George to me when he heard this. 'That's capped all! Best hoont I've been on for many a day!'

But the best specimens in the Major's collection were the home-raised moths. He had hunted under leaves on bushes and trees to find the small eggs, or the caterpillars themselves. These he kept in an open shed which he called his 'lavarium'. The caterpillars and the newly-hatched eggs were placed in gauze cages with a jar containing their particular food plant. He would send out an occasional urgent order for fresh poplar or aspen leaves, as these trees did not grow near his home. As the season progressed his 'zoo' became quite interesting. One game visiting schoolchildren used to play was 'find the stick caterpillars', for some of these would quickly disappear by pretending to be twigs on their food plant when alarmed.

Our favourite was the larva of the puss moth. It was so grotesque. It was large, green-and-chocolate coloured, and had a painted face, a hump, and an up-turned forked tail. When it was alarmed it reared up and two red threads were pushed out from its tail and lashed about. It was a miniature nightmare.

But all caterpillars are attractive in their way. They have such interesting ways of moving – smoothly with legs in unison like a pullman coach; or geometrically by moving back end up to front end, then moving up the front end after a tentative wave. Or they descend on silken threads by the score, covering one's clothing. I am always worried on arriving indoors to find these creatures about my person, for I must return them to nature and I can never be sure about which food plant they came off. Must I let them die of hunger?

Caterpillars, too, have such efficient ways of eating, from side to side in a continuous munch, starting left, finishing right, then clicking back like a typewriter carriage. During a 'caterpillar year' in a hardwood forest you can actually hear them eating on a still day, in their thousands. Sometimes the trees are stripped as if autumn has come early.

Raising your specimens from the larva stage, allowing them to pupate in their own way, then watching them eventually break out of their chrysalids with wrinkled wings which open up like umbrellas as they dry, is the best way to get perfect moths. It is certainly the best way to obtain the scarce ones, as you are protecting them right the way through their development from predators, from birds, from the dreaded little ichneumon flies which decimate the moth population by laying their eggs in caterpillars on which their own larvae finally feed. If you raise ten moths from a clutch of eggs you can then let eight go; where maybe only one, or two, would have survived in nature.

On another night I went bug hunting with a keen entomologist who had corresponded with the Major. We were walking through the wet mosses at dusk, netting the moths that rose from the thick growth at our feet. It was a good night for moths. What I took to be a very large one indeed flew between me and the darkening sky. I was getting good at netting by this time, pushing the net very rapidly behind the moth, swinging it downwards, and twisting the handle so that the insect was trapped in the fold of the net. I got this big one, and called to my companion to bring a large-size box and the lantern. To my great surprise I felt the net tug in my hands. A big one indeed!

By the lantern light I pushed the large pill box down into the net, but we could see nothing there. However the net was tangled and I carefully tried to disentangle it. Suddenly there was a movement and I felt something grip a finger. I went cold as I drew it upwards in something of a panic. Then in the light we saw what it was. I had caught a little pipistrelle bat. It had got tangled in the net, and its tiny feet had grabbed my finger in an effort to get out. I pulled the net folds away gently and lifted it up. It hung on my finger, upside down, for a second or two, then it spread its wings slowly, and took off into the night. In hunting moths I had caught another moth hunter.

By comparison with moth hunting, butterfly hunting can pall. There are only about seventy species in the British Isles, and when you have specimens of all those in your particular neck of the woods you have to travel farther afield. Or if you are a collector it is a matter of swapping a Lake District small mountain ringlet for a south of England chalkhill blue. But I am definitely not in favour of merely collecting. Collectors, of birds, of birds' eggs, as well as insects, have done terrible damage in the past. Collection-mad Victorians, and unenlightened game-keepers and their employers, have robbed us of much.

The small mountain ringlet butterfly, still living in one or two of the Lake District mountain areas, on some mountains of the Scottish Western Highlands, and a few places in Ireland, is a rare survivor from the Ice Age. The Lake District colonies, cut off completely from all others for many centuries, could soon be wiped out by over-enthusiastic collectors. The netted carpet moth, found only in the Lake District and in a place in North Wales, is another rarity. An acquaintance who calls himself a naturalist once proudly brought one in a matchbox to show me. The beautifully-patterned creature was, of course, dead. 'Netted it last night,' he boasted, 'in a spot I know. Just brought it in case you had not seen one before.' I damned him heartily.

The only excuse for collecting, in my opinion, is to obtain an appreciation and a study of the insect natural history of one's own area. The lepidoptera of other areas, and indeed other countries, are extremely interesting, but have no place in the collection of a field naturalist.

I recall one unusual phenomenon when I was butterfly hunting. I was walking with Buck among thistles in a sunlit glade in the wood when I saw a large fresh-looking butterfly on a thistle-head. It was a high brown fritillary. I took the net, stalked up behind it, and just as it moved off at high speed, swung the net quickly and got it. I turned the net over, took a pill box out of my haversack, then slid the box carefully into the net where I held the butterfly gently trapped. Just as I had the box within reach, and had loosened the net folds to push it closer, the butterfly began to struggle and then – it squeaked!

I was so startled that I dropped the box and allowed the creature to escape – which was probably just why the insect had made the noise. I have never heard or read of anyone else ever hearing a butterfly emit a noise.

The death's head hawk moth does squeak when captured. But then it is a large, fat, strong, macabre looking insect anyway, with the ominous likeness of a human skull patterned on its

back. If you had the courage to go so far as to try to box this creature you would half expect it to growl!

So, often, when sleeping out, my fondness for moths ruined my night's reading. If a big one hovered on to the candle flame, I could only blow the light out and hope that it got away unscathed.

17 Forest Fare

The word 'temple' comes from the root 'tem', to cut – a forest clearing. The inspiration of those who made civilization's first temples and churches all over the world, was the forest. You can see it in the pillars, the arched roofs, the decorated ceilings. For the gods walk in the forest. If you walk in alone, deep into the heart, you will feel their presence. They speak in the terrible silence. You may walk through the trees, down the naves, and suddenly, in this place of massive trunks, great brooding boughs, and below this spreading green canopy, you are about the altar. And you are really alone. Alone as a person in pain, or close to death. You do not quite know why this is the place. This glade of all glades. But you are suddenly an intruder. You walked into it the master of your fate. You had a purpose. You suddenly forget what it was. For a voice says, 'Be still.' And if you have the courage to heed, and wait, you will be on the brink of knowing.

When you reach the sacred sanctuary you may choose one of the three basic fear-reactions: to stay and worship; to leave well alone and go away; or to bring tools and cut it all down. Britain was once one huge forest; and these were the three reactions of the early settlers: the Celts, the Romans, the Anglo-Saxons. Now there is hardly any of the forest left, for the Anglo-Saxon in us, the extrovert with the slight touch of claustrophobia, is satisfied. We have pushed the fearful forest back. We have exterminated the bears and the wolves, and the dreadful forest bogey-men dare not wander into the Anglo-Saxon desert.

But the fear is still there, and sensible people must rationalize it. That tree in the garden, it looms hugely and darkly. We must cut off its limbs because it keeps the light out of the dining room. Or we must fell it, for the roots may undermine the house foundations, or they will get into the drains. The falling autumn leaves will block up the gullies and downspouts. Birds congregate on the tree and their droppings foul the car, or the washing. If all else fails, you may always call in an expert who will examine the tree carefully and tell you that it is unsafe. This final excuse is the favourite of our Local Authorities' Highways Committees, and the 'dangerous', the tottering poor invalid of a tree, is laid low with the help of a tractor, winch, power saws, and a squad of man. It takes them all day.

There were three ways in which primitive man could make a living for himself. He could be a hunter, a fisherman, or a nomadic farmer. So with the rest of his tribe he sought out the forest, the rivers or shores, or the fertile plains and sun-drenched hills. Modern man's annual holiday migrations, when he throws off his attachment to his largely artificial vocation to follow his natural inclinations, takes him to the water, which he sits by, swims in, or boats on. Or he tours, seeking the new pastures, through the valleys, up the hills and mountains. Few of us in Britain seek out the forests. But more of us will. The tide has already turned. The Forestry Commission is our largest landowner and new forests are beginning to take shape, and under the new enlightened policy the state forests are becoming places of recreation. Once we become more familiar with forests we shall lose that fear of the terrible unknown, and re-discover their fascination. Forests have one very large advantage over other recreation areas – they can absorb more people without getting crowded. That is important when there are so many of us living on so small an area.

But there are forests and forests. The lovely piece of wood-land that we find about the stately home, now, by the grace of God and the modern economic climate, mercifully open to the public – that is not a forest. A forest has depth. You walk through woodland. You walk into a forest. A hundred doors close behind. A hundred open up before. You are engulfed in an environment just as free and natural as the sea shore, or the mountain peak. There are three things that cut a man down to size – the sea, the mountain, and the forest. And there are three journeys that you can make towards self-knowledge, and to glimpse the immense reality of life – down to the sea, up to the mountains, or into the wilderness. But you must leave as much as possible behind.

The Great Wood was certainly a wilderness. I walked into a local pub one day and overheard two men talking.

'I was going by t'Great Wood. And out comes this girt dog-fox like a rocket, and nearly bowls me o'er.'

'Dog fox was it?' remarked his companion. 'Wouldn't sur-prise me if a rhinoceros came out of that place.'

George, too, told me that he always hated a hunted fox to turn into the wood.

'Why?' he exclaimed, 'I'll tell you why. Because the craggy place is as full of holes as a maggotty old cheese. And because if t'fox and hounds get amongst t'thick stuff you need a bloody crystal ball to know what's t'appen next. That's why.'

A forest is a carefully-balanced society of living things. The three elements – the plants, the animals, and the insects – are completely interdependent. If an old tree crashes at last to earth, the sunlight touches the floor through the open canopy and dormant seeds take root; and soon new saplings are reaching upwards to fill the gap. If one species of insect goes into a decline for some reason, another thrives to fill the niche that it leaves. If a certain animal population increases so will its predators, so long as man does not interfere.

But deer, now that the wolves are exterminated, have no real enemy but man. If a wood becomes overpopulated with roe, some will have the wanderlust and travel for miles. But while the pressure is on the territory, the bucks, more eager to assert their property rights, will do more damage to the young trees by increasing 'marking' activity, by fraying the bark. So in a commercial woodland it is necessary occasionally to cull. A very skilled job indeed, and not one for trigger-happy amateurs. Young bucks have a wanderlust when they are sizing up the lie of the land and deciding where to stake their claim. So, young as Buck was, he began to wander farther afield, though always returning to the shelter. But if I left that part of the wood he would follow.

One day I was working in the wood near the tarn boundary and decided to return to the shelter by walking along the road. I was surprised to find that Buck was walking along the verge behind me, as I thought that he had not been with me all day. There is a point where the road is below the level of the wood, which was on our right. To the left was a plantation with a deer fence. Just as we reached this point a car came bearing down on us at some speed. Buck panicked, made a move towards the deer fence, and checked. I called him and waved my arm towards our wood. There was a rock cutting about five feet high, surmounted by a wall of about four foot. Buck jumped, scrabbled for a hold on the rock, got it, and jumped again, touching the wall-top lightly with his feet before dropping into the wood. It was a magnificent acrobatic display.

The car stopped, and the motorist's jaw dropped open. 'That was a deer!' he exclaimed.

'Yes,' I said.

'But – you spoke to it. Told it to jump and it did.'

'Lucky it did,' I said. 'If it hadn't you might have run it down.'

I walked on for some distance and looked back. The car was still stationary. The driver was still gaping. I climbed into the wood.

I had improved my shelter by lengthening it. I had also made a bed by logging off a rectangle, and filling the space within it with spruce and yew tips, packed tightly together with their twigs thrust firmly into the soft ground. After a I had had a bit of practice at making this, it was as good as a spring mattress, and pleasantly warm and aromatic.

Food storage in the outdoors is a serious matter. I had to add a biscuit tin to my necessities so as to store the flour and salt away from dampness. Food must be kept off the ground where foxes, hedgehogs, voles and mice cannot reach it. A friend of mine once saw a vixen slouching along a hedge bottom dragging behind it a pound or so of sausages, no doubt to feed her cubs. Someone at the farm camp site, from the direction of which it was moving, would be cursing his folly at leaving food at ground level. No doubt the long-suffering farm dogs would be blamed. What fun those cubs would have had, falling on the sausage-string and worrying it, and pulling the raw meat out of the elastic skins!

I made a rough conical basket out of hazel and willow rods, and wedged it in an oak tree, which was as good a larder as I could improvise. I certainly lost nothing from it.

Opposite the entrance to the shelter I built a windbreak – a wide semi-circle of stakes driven into the ground, and interwoven with hazel and willow switches. This was my kitchen. At one end of it was my pride and joy – my oven. This was a construction of hard slates mounted on a hearth of stones. A stone flue behind the oven drew the fire backwards, so that the heat warmed the oven bottom and back. The whole was sealed off with blue boulder-clay from a beck bottom. The oven widened my menus considerably. I was able to make quite edible biscuits and pastry. I used the old country substitute for baking-powder – good white wood ash. That from ash wood was best. After some experience of the oven I could turn out an apple pie, not quite as nice as mother used to bake, but delicious all the same. I liked this oven so much that later I built another like it near the hut. I got far better results from it than from the nasty biscuit-tin type substitute that I had to stand on the gas ring.

I made several utensils out of wood. I made a spoon from a hazel rod – this needed very little making as the stem had grown flat at one end where it pressed against a neighbour, and it was almost spoon shaped to begin with. I had a number of forks from naturally forked sticks, and after discovering that green bird-cherry wood was almost as good as asbestos for being non-combustible, I made a gridiron of it, for broiling meat. I had a clothes-horse for drying washing and wet clothing, and airing blankets. I made a birch twig besom for keeping the area clean, and a slate cupboard to keep my books and candles and matches dry.

Any waste food, apart from bread and biscuit which Buck would eat, I scattered beyond the kitchen for the mice to enjoy. There was precious little beyond potato peelings. One morning I awoke to hear some chomping noises, peeped out and saw a hedgehog enjoying the handout. He came several times after that. There is something so endearing about the ugly creatures. They do not care a hang about making a noise and they grunt and snuffle about. They often have a runny nose and have a good sneeze. Their noses are extremely sensitive, which no doubt accounts for their moistness. They have to have a keen sense of smell to turn up insects and worms, which are the main part of their diet. To watch one chewing a slug noisily, with eyes closed in ecstatic appreciation of the delicacy, is one of the most stomach-revolting sights I know. People who have kept them in their gardens, almost as family pets, remark on their intelligence. They are certainly rather unpredictable. One will come to you at the same spot each night for tit-bits, another will show you utter contempt and ignore delicious cheese, a nice worm, cold rice pudding, or any other mouth-watering temptation. Some will uncurl at once when you stroke their nose gently, and enjoy the sensation like a kitten. Others do not even bother to roll up when they meet you. Yet others close up like a clam. They are acrobats. If they come to a steep bank which they wish to descend they often just go down head first, fall, and land at the bottom in a soft-cushioned ball. I once watched one climb the trunk of a leaning tree and get well into the branches, snuffling away after insects in the rotten bark. They have a fantastic gift of survival, and have been natives of Britain possibly longer than any other surviving mammal.

Another favourite neighbour was an old toad, who lived in a pile of stones near the shelter clearing. Like the hedgehog, he would make no attempt to escape when I stroked him affectionately on the nose. And he would sit there, like a fat buddha, waiting for his next meal to come within reach.

Came the day when I decided that I should repay the hospitality that some of my friends had shown me from time to time. I was determined to show them that I was not as un-civilized as they thought I was. I dragged in some logs which I placed along the wind-break. With my axe I cut the uppermost sides of them with a series of notches, then split along to them so that I had flat surfaces. They were quite comfortable benches. I acquired some jam jars and string, and put candles in them and hung them from convenient branches as lanterns. At the same time I made a concession to civilization by picking up my razor and soap, and using them. When I took a rare visit to town, to lay in some special supplies, I even had a haircut. I toyed with the idea of throwing away my disreputable ex-army combat jacket, but felt that that was going too far. Buck was already, I swear, giving me some old-fashioned looks.

Dave, George, Stanley and Billy agreed to come if I had a 'case o' brown'. Stanley said that he would bring a bottle of home-made rhubarb wine to help the dinner down, and George threatened to bring a 'drop of the real stuff'.

When the Saturday arrived I collected a dixie to make coffee

in, and some metal plates and mugs. In the afternoon I got the
oven going and made a successful, really thick apple pie. A deep
metal plate fitted snugly over it, and after the pie cooled, I fitted
it over, and stowed it safely in my tree. Meanwhile I had got a
good fire going in a deep trench I had dug by the side of the
kitchen. In it I heated some stones. Later in the afternoon I raked
out hot embers and stones, cleaned the stones, then lined the
bottom and sides of the trench with them. I then lined this again
with bunches of watercress, moistened in the stream, then into
this hot nest I laid some buttered and salted chicken halves,
topped them with cress and hot stones then a hot slate lid, and
covered it with soil and sods. I put potatoes in the embers at the
fire side, got the oven hot and made a biscuit dough; then
waited somewhat anxiously.

Luckily it was a fine evening and nothing was going wrong. I
tried to be as calm and as philosophical as Buck, who lay at the
end of the kitchen farthest from the fire, ruminating. I watched
his ears. Eventually one of them turned and he stopped chewing
cud. He listened. Then he rose to his feet, all attention, and I
knew that somewhere the lads were approaching. Buck moved
away silently and melted into the thicket before I heard Dave's
voice. He was the only one who knew the way, but he was
having his usual difficulty with clutching branches and root-
traps. The four of them were making a noise like a forest fire and
Dave sounded as if he was haranguing a revolutionary mob. But
Stanley's dog Judy came into view first, a bouncing little terrier
who, I was assured, had no truck with deer, knowing from sad
experience that they were not sporting enough to run at terrier-
speed.

Dave burst into the clearing declaring that he was hungry as a
hunter; but not before I had put the first biscuits into the oven.
Then we were all talking at once and I, and my way of living,
was the butt of the conversation. But I put a stop to it by throwing hot biscuits on to plates and passing them round, and putting more dough in the oven. Then, like a triumphant conjurer,
I dug away the soil above my trench with a slate, watched very
keenly by Judy, picked off the stones with a pair of wooden

tongs, forked away the cress and passed round the hot chicken halves. They received them in an astonished silence which I found very gratifying. I told them to help themselves to potatoes, stacked up more hot biscuits, then put the large apple pie back in the oven to warm. The rhubarb wine went down very well. It was, on George's reckoning, about twenty-five horsepower. Billy put it at a hundred and fifty per cent proof. It certainly made the dinner more exciting.

After a satisfying eating session I brought out my *pièce de résistance*, the warm apple pie, and we finished the lot off.

The rest of the evening passed off very well with beer and conversation. As dusk approached I lit my jam-jar lanterns, Stanley produced his mouth-organ and the woods echoed to hunting songs led by George's booming bass. It was surprising how time swept by, and when my guests left at last, swinging the lanterns with them on their strings, I felt that the whole episode had been a triumph.

When the last glimmer of their light had vanished, and their voices had died away, the darkness and the silence crept in around my single lonely candle and the embers of the fire. It fell around my shoulders like a welcome cloak. I sat in my favourite seat by the shelter and did nothing but gaze at the fire lazily. An owl cried nearby and was answered by another in the distance. It was time to turn in.

Although the trench and oven method of cooking was successful for most things, I had trouble with rabbits. They were easily obtainable from friends, but the meat is dry and the only way to cook them, in my opinion, is by stewing. Venison, which I could get cheaply if I had a mind to buy it, is also a dry meat. There are various recipes including the slashed meat with fat bacon one. Some use wines. We were discussing it over lunch one day in the forest, and George gave me the method.

'Put t'venison in a roastin' tin. Pour o'er it a glass of rum, a half o' barley wine, and another o' sweet strong cider. Pop t'lot in t'oven for an hour. Then tak it out and serve. The meat's still dry an 'orrible. You can throw it way. But, man! The gravy's marvellous!'

But to economize one had to use the rabbit glut, and I tried rabbit baked, roasted and pied; with onions and apples, herbs and spices. And this gave me a surfeit of skins. Now the Major had told me that the Red Indians used to cure animal skins by using the brains from the animal. They reckoned that each animal carried enough brain matter to cure its own skin. So I tried it. It is not easy to pull a skin off a rabbit without tearing it in some place. It needs practice. But the next job is more difficult. One has to scrape any flesh off the back of the skin, using a blunt knife. I used a flat piece of wood. The skin is very easily torn in this process. Next stage is to peg the skin to a frame so that it is stretched. The brains of the animal are mixed into a paste with a little warm water, and the horrible mess is rubbed well in. The skin is then dried on the frame in the sun. Preferably, I was told, high in a tree, as the blow-flies never fly high.

When the skins are dry the next process is to get them soft

and supple by working them in your hands. I tried hard at this but I never got a skin really supple. I stitched skins together until I made myself a rug for the bed. It looked very decorative but I am not sure that it served a useful purpose. But it proved that, at a pinch, if I wanted to extend the experiment of living outdoors with the least possible equipment, I could at least make myself – say – a sleeveless jacket. But I would have to hang it in woodsmoke for a long time to get rid of the rabbit smell.

Perhaps I took to living in the forest so well because some distant Celtic ancestors of mine were forest dwellers. But they could never have been far away from mountains and water. Somewhere, in all of us, there is a Robin Hood or a Maid Marion. It is a pity that on the whole we are a little frightened to let them out.

18 *Attitudes*

By mid-summer Buck's head was showing 'buttons', the first
year's beginning of antlers. I judged the deer to be above average in size and weight for his age, and he was certainly very fit.
His coat shone, and his baby-speckles were less pronounced. He
continued to be very active. In his play runs he was getting faster
and stronger. I had to return to the hut for a time to clear a
backlog of work there. This meant that I had to re-introduce
him to civilization. The first visitor to greet us was the tortoiseshell cat, which showed its delight at our return by pre-

senting us with a bank-vole, which it deposited, alive, on the hearthrug, where it remained, panting for a while, before disappearing behind the bookcase.

We had another visitor in the night. He arrived with something of a commotion. There was a bang which aroused me from a very deep sleep. I listened, but the noise was not repeated and I dropped off again. Come the dawn I discovered what the noise had been, for sitting on the cross-beam of the hut was a rather dumbfounded tawny owl. He was not looking my way so I cleared my throat and his head turned right round and two large eyes looked at me, and blinked in the sunlight.

When I got up I soon found out where the owl had entered, for there was a pile of soot on the hearth. He must have thought the chimney worthy of investigation. Odd feathers and droppings lying about showed that he had made some sorties towards the windows, as I slept, in the hope of escape. But he had completely missed the partly-open door.

He sat there on the rafter while I ate my breakfast, having apparently decided to ignore me completely. When Buck drummed in he merely turned his head slowly towards the door, observed him with disdain, ruffled his feathers then continued his wondering contemplation. He sat there all day. At the approach of dusk I decided I would have to get him outside. I opened the door as wide as it would go, stood on the table, and attempted to shoo the bird towards the obvious exit. His head turned and he regarded my signals with wide-eyed surprise. But he did not move. So I gave him a shove. With the same expression of surprise he moved his wings, rose a few inches into the air, then landed on my wrist. Then he squeezed – hard. I was astonished at the strength in that grip. It was like a vice. I shouted, 'Ow!' but he did not let go. He merely turned on the pressure a bit more. So, with him still clamped to my wrist, I jumped off the table and made for the door without delay. Once outside, his head turned round and upwards, looking for a line of escape, then he let go and rose silently, up, behind, and into the pines. And all that was left was the pain in my wrist, and a soft feather floating slowly downwards.

In the next few days we had a number of people making their way up the drive to the hut. An artist who wanted to sketch Buck. A teacher who wanted to bring his field-study group. I persuaded him not to. I could not face a whole group of sightseers. But I was not prepared to receive the red-faced, stoutish gentleman whom I found on my doorstep on returning from work. He was fanning flies away angrily and he began by asking me what I intended doing to compensate him for the damage that my roe had done to his garden. I recognized him then as a man who took a nearby cottage as a summer residence. It seemed that he went out into the garden one morning to find Buck finishing off the last of his rose buds after working his way along the row and seeing off the best part of a flower bed. He had thrown a stone at Buck and he had made off. I asked him if he was sure that Buck was the culprit. His answer was astonishing: 'Of course. *Wild* deer would hardly come into my garden. Would they?'

I asked why not. He spluttered that he had never heard of such a thing. I told him that all the gardens thereabouts were troubled with wild deer, and if he wanted to keep them out he would have to put up a six-foot fence. He said I was a liar. Wild animals do not go in gardens!

It took me a while to get some glimmer of understanding. Here was a man from some city, who had made a home of the cottage, had got landscape architects and contractors in to reshape and plant the piece of land that went with it, into a garden. He was obviously proud of it as being his own expensive creation. It was an extension of his home. Wild deer were creatures that lived in woods and you never saw them. It must have been my 'tame' deer that had violated his home. I repeated that he had only to ask around and all his neighbours would tell him that wild deer frequently entered gardens and did damage. It was something one had to live with.

He said, 'If you allow your deer to go about doing damage of this sort I shall get my gun and shoot it!'

At this I lost my temper and told him to go to hell; that I hoped his roses would develop tame mildew and blackspot, and that his flower beds would be eaten by tame rabbits from the fields, and that tame moles would destroy his lawn. He stomped off in a rage and left me with a black hatred that utterly destroyed the peace of the rest of my day. Later I felt pity, and some remorse at my unnecessary heat. For here was a city dweller, like myself, but a man who, far from getting away from it all, had brought it all with him. He carried a little invisible envelope of urban comfort and safety with him wherever he went. He was afraid of raw nature. A wild flower would doubtless be a weed. Any insect would be a pest. All I could wonder at was why he came at all.

This sort of attitude to wild nature, though, is not confined to town-dwellers. Many a countryman's first reaction on seeing a wild animal is to shoot it. It is bound to do harm to the farm or small-holding. I once met a farmer who boasted that he had shot a barn owl. When I asked why, he looked at me as if I was an ignoramus. 'Owls take chicks, don't they?'

What I find inexplicable is the country 'sportsman's' persecution of the badger. Some men will go to fantastic lengths to find setts, then laboriously dig them out, or let their terriers 'have a go'. Whenever I find a badger sett I keep the knowledge strictly to myself.

There is still some subconscious superstition behind some of the countrymen's attitude to wild life. When I told Mrs C. about the visit of the owl, next time I went down to the farm, she was horrified: 'There will be a death for sure!' I reminded her that she had promised all sorts of evil things about there being shrews in my home. 'How you live in that dreadful place I shall never know!' she said with some concern, and she told me that it was time I found myself a lady friend and went out more. 'I couldn't,' I said sadly. 'What with the shrews and the owl, who knows what dreadful calamity might descend on a woman who associated with me.' Mrs C. looked hard at me for a moment, then threw the dish cloth she was using. It was a good aim.

Mrs C. also had a deep respect for black birds – any of them. Crows, rooks and jackdaws about the place gave her 'the

creeps'. And she told a bloodcurdling tale about a jackdaw
which pecked at her aunt Alice's window for three days, and
one week later her uncle Stanley had a heart attack in the ship-
pon, and died. 'And he was such a fine-looking man.' Magpies,
too, one had to respect, and she recited the old country saw
'See one for sorrow; two for mirth; three for a wedding; four
for a birth; five for silver; six for gold; seven for a secret not to·
be told; eight for heaven; nine for hell; and ten for the devil's
own sel'.'

Dave told me that the rhyme had 'nowt to do with magpies.
In my family it were crows.'

Luckily for all of us one does not see ten crows together very
often. In fact when I told the Major that I could not always tell
the difference between crows and rooks at a distance, his advice
was: 'If you see one rook, it's a crow. If you see two crows,
they're rooks.'

The Major's attitude to the countryside, and nature, was unusual for a countryman born and bred. He was a hunting-shoot-
ing-fishing country gentleman, but he was also a keen naturalist.
He spent hours bird watching, and hunted for nests with the
enthusiasm of a schoolboy. His knowledge was considerable.
Not so much on the facts and figures. Many modern amateur
naturalists take pleasure in spending endless hours collecting
food for computers. This thrush's tail is eighty-one millimetres
long, or the average population of thrushes in a certain reserve
is one pair to five hectares. The amount of information gathered
in some areas around Field Study centres is such that there can
hardly be a bird without a ring on its leg. No doubt this research
is very necessary; but much of the work must be as dry and
dusty as looking at stuffed birds in an old museum. We must
measure this bird, this glorious free creature, weigh it, slap a
label on it and confine it conveniently to a tidy shelf of knowledge. This is fine for professional research; but one should never
impose such a narrow system of nature study on laymen, and
particularly young students. How many of us, in childhood,
have suffered under the hands of an English teacher, trying desperately to make us appreciate Shakespeare by having us learn

by heart the plea of Portia in the Court of Justice in *The Merchant of Venice* – mercilessly, and with the maximum amount of strain.

The too intensive study of one part; of a Shakespeare play, or of nature, prevents a proper appreciation of the whole. While it must be valuable for a serious and aspiring artist to study the form and shape and construction of the left ear of a figure by Da Vinci, the earlier student must see the perfection of the whole, and realize that the whole could only be thus, and that it is this wholeness that the artist would want us to appreciate. While one can study, with profit, the part of one instrument, in one part of a movement in a great symphony, it is the way that it fits into the pattern and harmony of the whole that stirs and moves us.

Here is a foxglove. It is a common thing. But in form and shape and colour, and with those delicate markings within the flower, it is just about the most marvellous thing that one could possibly meet on a woodland walk. It is worthy of close examination. But it is the fact that it is there; among the ferns close about this crumbling fallen tree; surrounded by legions of its kin glowing through the glade in mauve drifts in the sunshine-shafts that break through those great lichen-speckled oak trunks; under the green frondose clouds that stir to the west wind and are filled with blackbird song, that is important. It is the pulsing, breathing, thrusting life; the wholeness; that pours in on your senses. It is the impression of a perfect wholeness that can lift you up to a higher, shining level of consciousness.

One foxglove can say, 'I live!' and one can glory in it. But it is the harmony of the whole that cries out, 'This is what life is about: a close dependence upon one another; a struggle here; a triumph there; a death that opens up a door to life; a decay that nourishes; a sacrifice; a waiting; a sleeping; an awakening; an opportunity; a falling; a climbing; a sadness; a joy. And more. It is there before us like a great book, and if we spend too long in analysing, and learning by heart one meagre sentence of it, we might as well have stayed shut up in the airless comfort of our brick and concrete cells and gone on vaguely pretending that the world is just one huge automated factory that can go on producing wealth as long as we can master the formula.'

The Major was interested in the thorough exploration of the whole of his own locality. Each new discovery was exciting because it opened up new territories of further discovery. Probably the only thing we had in common, coming as we did from backgrounds that were poles apart, was a keen interest in living things. But I learned this from him: that any given field of study is not just a confined fragment of space. It cannot be separated from infinity. One can take a powerful microscope and begin with the simplest, tiniest forms of life; from these to the smaller animals and simple plant forms; through the larger plants, insects, mammals and birds; and then so on into outer space with a telescope.

And the whole of this turning in time. Infinity in eternity.

What can add most to the appreciation of life is that sense of being poised in infinity. A part of nature. One winter evening I was walking down Oxford Street in London, watching the hurrying and worrying passers-by and thinking what a hurly burly of miserable madness it all was, when up above the great stone and concrete cliffs there was a pale portion of moon; and stars. I was instantly reminded that the same moon and stars were shining, at that moment in time, on the levels of the lake and the white-capped hills of home. And I remembered that men are animals, and that each animal which hurried by filled its little place in the purposeful scheme. A city is a sort of human ant-hill. There is nothing necessarily mad about ant-hills.

It was people like the Major who helped to fire my enthusiasm for seeing and enjoying living things. Although with fellow entomologists he used the Latin names of insects, when he spoke to a layman like myself an '*Arctia caia*' would be a 'tiger moth', and his eyes would light up with excitement as he showed and explained to me the variations in colouring in the specimens that he had. He was at his happiest when he was showing off his caterpillar zoo to visiting children. There are others who have passed on their enthusiasm to me. The ornithologist, who was in private life an accountant. The man who, when he was not watching deer or badgers, tried hard to be a policeman. Happy men all. The wife of the latter man told me that when the birth of her first-born was imminent, she half-expected the child to have antlers.

Dave's passion was for timber, but it was a passion he was strangely half-ashamed of. He would take off to drive fifty or more miles to see, ostensibly, some distant relation; but in fact he would detour to take in a fine stand of Douglas fir some-one had told him of; or a rare tulip tree; or he would return with some hazel rods for stick making, 'as straight as billiard cues'. Farmers and shepherds for miles around held great store by Dave's sticks. Most of the sticks exchanged hands in the Punch Bowl on a Saturday night. Some of them were works of art, the crook being made of ram horn, fitting tight to the stick with a deer-antler collar. He was also quite a good wood carver. He would pick up an odd piece of timber stock, which he kept in a shed, turn it in his hands, and would say, 'there's a salmon', or, 'there's a weasel' in the wood. Sometimes though, half-way through the carving, he might change his mind. But the result was always good. It was the look of the grain, and the feel of it in his hands, that absorbed him; as well as the sight of a fine tree.

I suppose my main interest was in botany. I have a list still of the flowers and plants I noted in the local exploration. Exclud-ing trees and shrubs they number a hundred and thirty-two. There must be many more unrecorded. But looking through that list now brings happy memories. I think my best find was the columbine: right in the heart of the wood where it could not possibly have been a garden escape. Hearts-ease is not all that rare a plant, but when I discovered this beauty it might have been a rare orchid. Among the commonest plants were butter-wort and sundew, the insectivores. These small plants do not usually attract a second glance. The first has fleshy sticky leaves to which flies become attached and are held fast while the leaves curl around them to extract nourishment. The second, in the mass, and shining in the sunlight, is a glowing bed of fire. One could just pass them by, assuming that they were some kind of moss. A closer look reveals them as short plants with red, very hairy leaves, each hair-tip holding what looks like a spotlet of dew. But this tempting drink for insects is a glue. Once the insect is caught there, the leaf closes about it slowly and absorbs nourishment.

At one time the sundew was a valued herb, said to hold the secret of youthfulness. Another favourite of mine is the scarlet pimpernel. Its flowers are so bright and smart. It used to be called the poor man's clock, because it was said, although I never checked this, that the flowers open at seven in the morning, Greenwich Mean Time, and close at 14.00 hours. It was also considered to be a good remedy for the bites of vipers. A tincture of a decoction of pimpernel, though, could cure anything from insanity to dimness of sight. I must have a weakness for the small plants, for another favourite is herb robert – it almost rivals gorse for a long flowering season, and in autumn the leaves shine red. But undoubtedly the flower of the Lake District is the daffodil. Every April they come to us like a miracle in great yellow clouds. But they, and the primroses that are given to us later, suffer from the vandals with trowels and bags; even occasionally with spades and vans. It used to surprise me that the sheep, which heaven knows eat practically anything, left the daffodils. But the fact that the old herbals list its properties as emetic explains all.

Plant hunting is a fascinating business. Our ancestors knew the wild plants better than we do. For practically every one offered a medicine, or a cleaning or preserving material, or a dye. How this was discovered suggests hundreds of dangerous experiments. Often it was thought that God, in his wisdom, provided the remedy for all man's ailments in his natural garden. Each plant suggested the ailment it was designed to remedy, by its shape and colour. The broad, spotted leaves of the lungwort suggested lungs blotched with infection. The bright white flowers of eyebright suggested that they were a gift to those with failing sight. The deep red veins on the leaf of the bloody-veined dock suggested that the plant could be valuable in stopping bleedings. The fleshy flat leaves of the liverworts certainly suggest liver, and were used for jaundice and liver complaints. The odd thing was that quite a lot of the old remedies actually worked. A good many of them are still used in this sophisticated age of synthetics.

19 *Autumn*

Late summer brought the stormy weather. Wind and pelting rain flogged the trees and brought green leaves down like tattered rags. Buck, like all animals which rely on hearing to warn them of danger, was restless and uneasy when the wind blew. The noise as the wind thrashed through the trees was like heavy sea-breakers and the backlash of heavy-leaved branches was like the smashing of sea-shore pebbles. The total effect was deafening and as the storm persisted there grew a steady background roar of flooded becks.

The rain never bothered Buck, though it flattened his head hair ridiculously and he looked like a naughty boy who had been playing with his big brother's brilliantine. But the noise worried him so much that he sought my company and came indoors, taking his old bed on the hearthrug, and chewing fitfully at his cud, ears moving uncomfortably with every new roar.

I do not like the wind either. When it was at its worst in the forest by night I would toss about uneasily on my bunk and dream that I was at sea again, and give thanks, when it woke me, that I was not. On the fells wind is almost noiseless – a wild hissing as it flattens the grasses. But it is the pressure of it rushing past one's ears that is discomforting; and their gale, unchecked by branch or leaf, is unmerciful. Many a time, on reaching exposed places, I have had to stagger along, crouching and resting by stages. I have been knocked down by wind countless times and once I was picked up by a northeaster and lifted several yards.

It was a terribly windy day for the sale at Parkerground. Dave called and said that he and Billy would be going as Billy was keen on buying a large hen-house which would make a fine garage and workshop for his motor-cycles. There was also a wide range of fascinating bargains. He was hoping that I was interested as they would need a lift with the henhouse if they bought it. He had borrowed a lorry from a local carrier.

The sale took place in an implement shed, out of the wind. The lanes around the farm were choked with cars and vans, and there was a good crowd of farmers, mainly after stock. We looked at the hen-house, which had been dismantled and was leaning against a barn wall. The wood, Billy pointed out, was sound. Not a sign of worm or rot – just wholesome creosote and hen dung.

We had to wait a long time for the hut to reach the head of the list, and Billy bid for it successfully. Then, to the surprise of Billy and me, Dave started the bidding for a piano. In fact he finished the bidding too, for no one else made an offer. It was knocked down to Dave for ten shillings. It was probably, Billy said, all that it was worth. Dave admitted that he had not examined it, but he thought it would please his sister, as she had always fancied one in the living room. And if it was no good he had not lost much. He also bought a radio for half a crown.

At the end of the sale we put the piano on the lorry first, with the help of planks and brawny jovial neighbours. But the hen-house was a different proposition. The sections were not too heavy, but they were unmanageable in the gusty winds which swirled around the barn buildings. All would be well, Dave explained, if we carried the sections horizontally to offer the least resistance to the wind. But it was impossible to lift them horizontally, for no sooner had we lifted than the wind tilted them one way or the other. If the section was tilted towards the wind, a gust would thrust it down suddenly and pin it firmly to the ground, wrenching arm-sockets. If it was tilted up, the wind would rush underneath and try to lift it bodily over, while Dave swore roundly, Billy set his mouth in a hideous grin of exertion, and I danced wildly in an effort to keep feet on terra-firma.

While the sale field emptied of buyers and sightseers, the three of us were left to struggle with this wild, bucking, wooden monster. We got one of the end sections on to the lorry by some fluke, but it had to stand on its side and be firmly lashed to both lorry and piano. We were doing fine with the second end until the wind whipped it upright, and to save it from turning right over and possibly smashing, we ran with it. We charged down that field like a schooner in full sail, bounding in great strides at a fantastic speed that took us right past the lorry, until finally the wind won its fight and pitched the section over. We fell on top of it, and scrabbled about on its malodorous surface in an attempt to hold it down. When we had more or less collected ourselves Dave said, 'Wait for a lull in the wind, and when I say "lift", lift the beggar and run for it.'

This we did, but to get back to the vehicle we had to run against the wind. After a grim struggle in which all three of us were performing somersaults, and other wild acrobatic feats worthy of a first-class circus, I had a brainwave. We tied a rope round the thing and dragged it behind us. We did this, too, with the other sections and the floor, and at last, covered in perspiration and reeking of hens, we tied on the lot and drove away.

We had more sense than to try to erect the hut at Billy's place. We put it off until the following evening. Before we attempted to tackle the piano, we had a wash and a meal, then over to Dave's.

Dave's sister, the great cake-maker, was a surprise. I had expected a well-built, cheery, rosy-cheeked country-wife. She was slim and pretty, and well spoken, looked you right in the eye when she spoke to you, and smiled a lot. When she laughed it was like music. Dave was proud of her.

'I've bought you a piano in the sale, love.'

'Piano? Sale? You must be daft.'

'It was a bargain. Couldn't resist. Show us where you want it. Look at the wood! Beautiful walnut!'

Dave's mother appeared from the stone porch, wiping her hands on her apron. She lived up to the country-wife image.

'A piano? Lad what next! You'll need to tak t'wall down to get it in.'

We went indoors and had a conference. The piano would stand against the wall opposite the door after we had moved the settee, and the whatnot, and a pot plant. We cleared a way through, and went out and removed the ropes, and the sacks that Dave had put around the tie-points to protect the precious wood. Two planks were brought from a shed and put in position, then we spat on our hands and started the 'Yo-heave-ho'. After Dave had suffered numerous injuries to various parts of his anatomy, and had to put up with the severe frustration of not being able to swear about it because of the female onlookers, we got it as far as the front porch.

Every Lake District cottage has a porch. It is where you drop your wet boots, waterproof, your stick or your tools, before venturing into the clean interior. But they are a severe handicap to furniture removing, particularly when the furniture has to go indoors at an angle to avoid the immovable battleship of a sideboard. But eventually the manoeuvre was accomplished, and we celebrated our success with a cup of tea. Then Dave put a chair in front of the instrument, lifted the lid to expose the yellow and black keys, and struck a chord.

'It wants tuning, of course,' he said needlessly. 'But I'll give thee all a tune before passing among you with me cap.'

He started to play a piece that Betty, at the Punch Bowl, had taught him. It defied description as a piece of music, but the exaggerated flourishes and the confident finger work produced some excellent entertainment which brought tears of amusement to his mother's and sister's eyes. And then I noticed the laughter stop and they looked at each other uncomfortably. Billy, who was standing with one arm on the piano, looked at me with his wooden, expressionless face, and I noticed a flicker of puzzled uneasiness in his eyes. Then I knew why, for drifting towards the corner where I was sitting was a strange, insidious, foul smell; a sour smell like very mouldy cheese; yet also strangely and more subtly noisome, reminding one vaguely of ill-kept knackers' yards, bloated dead fly-blown animal bodies on a hot day, and blocked sewer pipes.

Dave stopped playing suddenly.

'By George what a smell!' he gasped. 'Close the door somebody. Tom Poss must be muck-spreading.'

We went outdoors to investigate. There was no smell there and when we went indoors again, the smell appeared to have dispersed. Dave started at the piano again and the smell returned as strongly as before, like a fetid noxious gas.

Dave stopped playing as the awful truth was realized. We lifted the lid, and the smell rose so strongly that it sent us all rushing to the door for air. In the light of day we looked at each other with mouths open. Then Dave dived furiously into a shed and came out with a torch. We returned bravely, and we shone the torch down into the works. There were no dead rats, nothing to account for the smell. Indeed it had subsided again, and it would appear that it only materialized when the keys were struck. We took the front off the instrument. It was dusty, but there was nothing which could account for the smell at all.

Angrily Dave struck all the keys at once. It came at us, bursting like some hideous invisible bomb. We hurled ourselves out of the room again, stumbling through the porch and gasping for pure air in the yard outside.

Then Dave's mother began laughing. His sister began laughing. Billy's body began shaking. His shoulders began moving up and down. There was a wide-eyed helpless look in his eyes and tears started to trickle down his cheeks, he folded in the middle and out of his slot-like mouth came a weird, tortured sound: 'A-harr. A-harr. Oh! Oh! A-harr.' Then we were all throwing ourselves around in paroxysms of hysterical laughter. The two women were locked in each other's arms. Dave was leaning against the wall, yelling with laughter, and beating the stones with his fists. I collapsed on a rustic seat, holding my stomach and struggling for breath like a drowning man. It went on and on until I thought I was going to do myself some internal damage. Then very gradually it subsided. Dave said, 'My lord, what can it be? The damn thing must be haunted!' This set us all off again and it was a long time before sanity returned.

At last the women announced that the piano would have to go. 'It's all right so long as you don't play it,' argued Dave feebly. 'It's a nice bit of walnut.'

'Out!' said the ladies. So out it came again and was banished to an outshed, where so far as I know it could be to this day, for it would need a man of steely courage to attempt to break the thing up.

I went home (with a large piece of cake) thinking that this was the end of an eventful day. Something attempted, something done. But when I was resting by the fire, it being now a cool evening, I began to itch. I remembered that I had been scratching, on and off, through the last few hours, but now, in inactivity, it was getting unbearable. I tried to read, unsuccessfully. Then after suffering for too long I got lots of water in pans on the fire and the gas ring and tore off my clothes. My body had numerous red blotches, and I began to worry, trying to remember if I had had measles when I was a child. I felt better after a stand-up bath and a good rub-down. I thrust all my clothing in the linen basket.

I felt all right the next morning, and when Dave called the mystery was solved.

'By George, the hen-fleas off that hut gave me what-for yesterday!' he moaned.

Not all weather is stormy at the approach of autumn. Summer is reluctant to leave the Lake District. It says farewell so many times, like a veteran actor announcing a definite last appearance, it goes off to a noisy finale from the north and west winds: and then there it is again next week, as warm and sunny and friendly as if it had never been away. Visitors are surprised. They leave autumn elsewhere and find the Lake District still in summer green.

The first signs of autumn are chill temperatures in the evening and morning, with the tendency to mist in the lower levels. Then, in full day, the country begins to glow. The great slopes of bracken begin to brown like a crusty loaf. The geans, indistinguishable in the general green only days ago, burn yellow and red. Copper and mottled-green cascades fall from the beeches with each breath of wind. The larches pale to platinum, and the rowans light their lanterns of berries. Then a hundred shades of green and yellow and brown and red are kindled by the mellowing autumn sun.

The Celts, who knew and loved natural beauty, sang of a land of breath-taking loveliness where souls go after they have left the mortal body. A land where everything is fair, and there is no unhappiness, and no one ever grows old. Only the dead may see it; but it is just possible – just possible – for it to be seen by some chosen mortals. Perhaps some spirit may lead them there. And provided they are content to gaze and take nothing from it, they can return to mortality, to try to tell what is beyond all telling.

Go up into the fells early on a fine autumn morning and you can be one of the fortunates. Climb up above the grey mists and on to the sunlit slopes, then look down. The mist lies now like a great golden sea. Then wait. The veil dissolves and the colours begin to filter through. Then, at some mysterious bidding, the mists clear; and it is there below you, the radiant steeps tumbling down to the incandescent plain and the shining levels of water. Avalon, the fair land. The Mag Mell, the plains of happiness, where there is no more mourning, no grief, no pain. The land of eternal youth. So beautiful that the mortal eye cannot take it all in. So beautiful that the greatest poet that ever lived could never capture one fragment of it. It would flow away through the gaps and holes and mesh of mere words like water through a net.

Stay and look. Be still. Let there be no conversation. No sound to spoil the muted music which you will surely hear. Let there be no selfish thought. No thought of yesterday or tomorrow, or the last instant or the next. Live in this moment. Rest easy in it. For you will be the fortunate; glimpsing immortality.

If because of age or infirmity we cannot climb the fell; if, too, our senses are dulled to the sensations of the mortal dimensions of the world around us here in this glade; even then we can see the blessed land, if we take the path of the shining ones; the little people. It is there at our feet where the pendant dew-jewels light the bright green grass, and where weightless webs breathe in the wind. A tree stump covered in moss; take a close look, kneel if you must. The moss becomes a great jungle of fronds, each one a miracle of design. Their flowers hang like lanterns. Look here at the lichen; tiny rough grey-green stems, but moving closer we can see clusters of scarlet flower-heads like burning embers. See here the orange-yellow branches of fungi like the discarded antlers from a golden hind. And perhaps about you, pushing through the blazing leaf-litter, you can find the *clavaria*, the fairy clubs, delicate stems tipped with orange, or yellow, or brown. Journey with your eyes through this little Eden, then stand and look again. What you thought was mere earth, lit by the sun, has become transfigured. Hold on to that moment for you have become one of the fortunates.

You say perhaps that this is romantic nonsense? That when we look at the natural world, even in the near-magic of autumn colour, our impressions can only be subjective? We who are so heavy with thoughts of getting and spending, cannot look at it all afresh, like a child? But you must become as a little child to enter this Kingdom. It is not difficult. It is only a matter of putting aside all selfish thoughts; the cares of yesterday and the worries about tomorrow, and sitting silently and still in this one moment. It is not difficult. Only for one moment. And you can never be quite the same again.

I like autumn. It is the time when all the wild creatures are fat. The old hedgehog has put on enough weight to last him through a winter sleep. The red squirrels are deliriously wondering what to do with all the hazel-nuts that they cannot cram immediately. The wood pigeons are so full of acorns they can hardly take off; and the blackbirds stuff away the soft berries like naughty little boys at tea-parties. Buck did well, too, that autumn. I watched with admiration as he walked round a crab-apple tree and ate every windfall, and every hanging fruit within reach. I tried one bite and I thought the top of my head was coming off. Sloes are just about the most acid fruits that could torture your palate. Buck ate them greedily. I was told that roe find the fruit of rowan irresistible. I led Buck to a heavily loaded specimen and said, 'Eat!' and I took a handful for myself. He nibbled experimentally. Whether or not he had already eaten his fill of something else, I do not know, but he plainly did not care too much for those rowan berries. Which was strange

because I find a few quite palatable. Similarly with elderberries. Yet I can eat these by the handful. Roe seem to be partial to anything acid. Buck always enjoyed sorrel, which tastes rather like strong vinegar. And those crabs! The mere thought of it makes me drool uncomfortably.

I also like the smell of autumn. It is a clean, moist, piquant quality that defies description. And it means relief from the hay fever that has made my nose run like a hedgepig's all summer.

20 Departure

Winter is the busy time of felling and planting in the forest. There were some trees to fell in the early part of that winter, not far from my shelter. Some of the felling was done by ourselves; but the main part was done by contractors, a gypsy-like race of men who moved about the country, felling and hauling. They were taking away the big stuff; we were felling timber we required mainly for our own use for fence-post making. Oak makes the best posts, though European larch is a good second as it is so resinous that it is very rot-resistant.

The first step in felling is to cut away the buttress at the base of the trunk with an axe. Then, having decided on which way the tree is to go; which depends to a great extent on which way it is leaning naturally, and on the side bearing the greatest weight; a cut is 'set in' on the side to which the tree is to fall. Then the tree is sawn, very close to the ground so as to prevent wastage, on the opposite side. When the saw is nearly through it is necessary to watch the tree top for a sign of movement; when it starts to go the saw is removed, there is a warning shout, and the fellers step back and to each side – never directly to the rear, as often when the tree falls it pivots on its branches and kicks back with its bole.

The felling of the tree is the easiest part. The 'dressing up' of the trunk, removing the branches, is more difficult as the cuts are awkward, and the grain gnarled and knotted. One can get into a tangle with the lot unless the limbs are pulled away as quickly as they accumulate. It is necessary to get a large fire going to consume the rubbish as quickly as one cuts it.

October and November often bring many hours of sunshine. I was tempted by good weather to return to the shelter yet again. It saved journeys and I could also make good use of the large fires. I hate wastage. One use was suggested by some after-dinner reminiscences of the Major. After using the large hot fire to cook my supper, I poked and pushed the blaze well back, and on the ground where it had stood I swept the embers back, too, with my birch-twig besom. I then made my bed on the warm ground. The first experiment taught me to move the fire back about an hour before turning in. Otherwise I felt like a rasher of bacon in a frying pan. On some early mornings of frost, when cold woke me up, it was necessary to rise, rake and sweep the still hot fire back to its former position, then lie on the ground from which it had just been moved. This under-floor central heating was most certainly a success.

By this time Buck had lost his summer coat, and all his baby speckles, and had taken on his thicker grey winter coat. The difference at first was quite startling, but the sleek new coat was certainly very smart. Winter did not bother him one bit. He always seemed able to find food among the undergrowth, in the grass glades, and in the swamps. And he could always come to me for a bread hand-out. He would now be absent at times for two days, but if I chose to look for him he was seldom very far away. When I returned to the hut he was often in his favourite spot on the bank above it. He was there when we had the first snowfall. It was short-lived, but while it fell it came in thick. I looked for Buck when the storm abated, and there he was, cud chewing on the bank, his coat plastered with snow, but quite unperturbed.

Over the next months I had to be absent for long periods. It was disturbing, but necessary. I was worried a little about Buck, but he was now quite capable of looking after himself. Dave would keep an eye on him. We also had some allies in a group of rover scouts who owned a hut on the edge of the wood. This was a self-built, heavy timber structure. They had roofed it, first with corrugated iron, then over that a thick layer of turfs to add heat and sound insulation, and to make the hut less ugly. Now this turf, for some reason, grew lush grass, and scores of birch seedlings took root in it. It was a simple matter for Buck to leap on to the low-hanging roof and feed away happily. The picture was bizarre – a deer feeding on a roof around a smoking stovepipe. The first time it happened was in the early light of dawn and the young men were awakened by the clump of the jumping deer, and then the strange noise of movements above. When they had recovered from their astonishment they became the deer's friends, and if there was nothing to cadge from me, if it was in a cadging mood, it could always wander down to their hut.

On my returns Buck would never come at me like a dog would, with obvious recognition and delight. I would return to the hut, and there would be no sign of him. Then when I was moving about with logs and kindling to get some warmth in the empty place, he would silently appear to watch. If I walked into the wood he would follow as if I had never been away, casually, browsing as he came. Sometimes he would come in and take his usual place on the hearth rug. I often had his company on the long dark evenings. We had no conversation, nor did he look me in the eye as a dog or a cat would. But he sought my company and I was grateful for it. I would sit on one side of the hearth with my books, Buck on the other, and there would be no sound but the hissing and cracking of timber on the fire, and the spluttering of the gas, and outside, perhaps, the cries of the tawny owls.

My absences grew longer. I saw Buck and my friends infrequently, and then in the spring I returned for a longer stay on a day of heavy downpour. I walked up the track to the hut, and the visibility in the streaming rain and the heavy wet mist was poor. As I approached the hut, suddenly Buck was there. Or was it Buck? A fine, full-grown specimen of a roe. Still in winter grey, and with a pair of single antlers still covered in velvet. I called to him. He stood above me on the bank, hesitated, then came down. His head hair was plastered with rain, and he shook it as he came, muffle quivering. He stood close to me and we breathed into each other's faces; then he followed as I went to the hut. When he came in I was better able to judge his new size. He appeared to have grown almost beyond recognition. He stood then two feet high and was well-fed and sleek.

It was good to be back in the old place. Next day the sun shone and the fat buds were bursting everywhere. I explored the wood again with Buck close behind. It was good to be alive. I climbed up to the great crag and looked down and out at the view again, patterned with varied greens and moving cloud shadows. There was the old familiar sound – the taut 'scree!' cry of the buzzard. I looked up, and there was a pair of them gliding effortlessly, circling about each other in a glad air-dance. Some would have it that wild creatures are incapable of emotion and therefore cannot feel joy. It is a lie. Many birds play with air currents. Foxes, otters, and badgers play hilarious games. Deer, wild ponies, and hares certainly run for joy. One day I watched the peculiar antics of a crow and a rabbit, dancing and sparring round each other for quite a while. It could only have been some sort of game. Many animals and birds must make the occasional discovery that they are fully alive. They must feel at times more intensely the vigorous flow of life within them. They must express their exuberance in some way. Much bird song is sheer excess of spirits. It is the natural animal joy of healthy youthfulness. Even elderly humans can feel this exciting awareness of the life-flow; especially in spring!

We made a wide circle of the wood, walking along the ridge to North Rock, then dropping by the boundary near the tarn, and back through Galleons Glade. We stopped there among the silent squadron. The only movement was from a tiny goldcrest, our smallest bird, even smaller than a wren, which was busily searching the branches and twigs. Beyond the glade we discovered, round a rotten birch stump, a beaten path. Roe had hammered this out, in love play the previous season, but I am sure from exuberance since. It is odd that these rings are invariably made round some prominent object, I once found a heavily-used one beaten round an old discarded bath-tub in a woodland clearing. Then I went back through the hardwoods; the sycamore buds were bursting, birches a bright-green mist, hawthorns well leafed. The rowans were grey with fat buds that I pulled off and chewed. They have a pleasant taste of almonds. The young alder leaves were shiny bright and Buck pulled at them as we passed. And as we neared the hut again I heard a cry which brings me joy each year the first time I hear it – the bubbling spring cry of the curlew.

That was one of my last long visits. I returned several times during the year that followed, but only for a few days at a time. I saw Buck on each occasion. By summer his antlers had lost their velvet covering and were bright and sharp. My friends kept me up to date on his activities. On one occasion he had attacked a neighbour's child. I do not know why. It might have been some movement on the child's part that suggested aggressiveness and brought the inevitable reaction. On the other hand my experience with Buck was that harmless play could often turn to rough stuff. I would never attempt to play the pushing game with him now he had his antlers. I had to pull him off from pursuing a friend who had started such a game and realized his error. I could see the potential danger in Buck's familiarity with humankind. Indeed I had seen it from the beginning. It was a worry that I had tried to push on one side. As it happened, in this incident the child was unharmed.

On one of my visits a mongrel dog, with a deal of some sort hound in it, made a rush at Buck and he ran off into the wood with the dog in close pursuit, growling and carrying on loudly. They were gone for some time. Then Buck reappeared. He was hardly blown – just showing signs that he was beginning to warm up. I thought he might be terrified of the hunting dog, for he had certainly taken off in a panic. I was surprised, and a little frightened then, when I saw the dog coming after him, still thirsting for blood. But Buck turned and stood still. He stamped one foot and his hair rose. Then he charged. The dog braked hard. Luckily it stumbled when the deer made contact, and the pointed business-end of the antlers merely grooved its back. But the impact was enough to send the dog rolling. Once clear it gave one yelp and was away with its tail between its legs with Buck still in pursuit. Buck did not respond to my call. It was some time before he came back to me, grazing casually. I later found that the dog was none the worse, but it had no doubt learned its lesson.

Some men on a building site nearby also told me that Buck would often put in an appearance to see how their work was progressing, and to see if there was any chance of an odd slice of bread. One day, the men said, they heard an approaching hullaballo and towards them came Buck with a mature roebuck on his heels. The roebuck caught up and 'gave Buck a pasting', apparently in its fury completely oblivious of the workmen until they ran forward to rescue Buck. Buck had obviously trespassed on the mature roebuck's territory, and this could hardly be tolerated from a young upstart who was not yet tough enough to establish a breeding territory of his own. The fact that Buck had returned to the building site was a little curious. The workmen had it that he had brought his aggressive rival purposely that way so that he could be rescued. They reckoned that he was on his way to being killed. More likely, I thought, he regarded this, which was not far from our hut, as his home territory; for this was his stand, and a roe often returns occasionally to the place where he was born and reared.

During the winter months roe often join forces and move about in groups, the males tolerating each other's presence in the mutual effort to protect and feed themselves. I never knew if Buck ever made a friendly contact with his own kind. During my winter visits again that year and early in the next he always approached me. If he had been with his fellows, of course, they would have kept clear of the scent of humans anyway. One of my visits there coincided with heavy snow, and when Buck came to me we followed his tracks back to see if he had been with a group. The tracks led to the southern end of the wood to a place know as Yew Crags. Snow was patchy here under the thick growth of the evergreen yews. There were tracks about, but it was not possible for me to decide whether or not they were all Buck's. It was likely, I thought, that there had been other roe there as it was an ideal place for wintering roe to hide out. Yew is poisonous to some animals, including cattle, but roe, I have observed, eat it with impunity; and often quite greedily. Indeed, posterity was almost cheated of a young yew tree I planted in a garden, when a roe almost completely devoured it, together with a neighbouring laurel bush, one hungry winter's day.

Another spring came. Buck now stood well over two feet high and his antlers, in velvet, each had three points, the lower ones pointing forward, the two upper ones upwards and backwards. Buck backed off angrily when I tried to examine them closely. There was very little 'pearling'; the knobbly roughness that distinguishes the antlers of a mature animal. But when the velvet had gone Buck would be pretty savagely armed. I was worried.

In the next visit in the early summer I did not see Buck. I checked with Dave, who told me that he was still about, but not seen as often, and he suggested that Buck might be 'doing a bit o' courting somewheres'.

I saw Buck once more in the early autumn. He was now a fine animal. He came as I was gathering wood for the hut. But he had strangely changed. I find it impossible to say how. The renewal of contact had always been casual. This time he refused the food I offered him, would not enter the hut, but took his favourite place on the bank top. He stayed there through the middle of the day but by evening he had gone.

Before my next visit I wrote to Dave to say I was coming, and was filled with apprehension when I received a card in reply. It stated briefly 'Buck has been in trouble and has not been seen since. Will tell you all about it.'

I called on Dave as soon as I could, and he told me the story. One morning Buck had apparently travelled some miles, and had appeared, rather oddly, in the playground of the village school while the children were at play. The teacher in charge, seeing some possible danger in the situation, called the children indoors, then telephoned a local farmer. He captured Buck, tied a rope round his neck, and took him back to his farm. He tied him up in his barn and a message eventually reached Dave that the animal should be collected. But when he got there, which was on the following morning, the farmer showed him the place where he had tethered Buck. There was just a broken rope end. Dave said that he and other friends had made searches, but there had been no sign of the animal. I left Dave in some dejection. I searched the wood myself in the familiar places, but somehow now I never expected to meet him. I feared the worst. I had a feeling that he was dead, and I had no wish to pursue any enquiries which I felt sure would lead to a very painful conclusion. A conclusion which I had always feared. Friendships with wild animals almost invariably lead to tragedy.

There were so many reminders everywhere. I noticed one night, as I sat in my hut of so many memories, that the hearth rug was the worse for wear; there was a bald patch in the middle of it, and I felt a twinge of misery when I remembered that this was Buck's doing. For roe like to scrape away a bare patch of ground for their beds. I could not help leaving my rough door ajar – just in case, and I upset my food as I jumped round when it was suddenly flung open. But it was only a strong gust of wind. I passed his favourite patch of birch thicket; the rock slab he had tried to climb. Then once I saw a roebuck in front of me and called, 'Buck!' The beast bolted at once, and I knew it was another animal.

Strangely, too, there was the night in the city. It was very late and it was quiet as I took a side street short cut to the station. Suddenly I heard a slight, familiar, wonderful noise behind me, and again I jumped; because I heard the sound of Buck's hurrying feet. I turned, and saw an empty milk carton pattering its way along the wall behind me in the wind. It is not easy, being a countryman.

More about Penguins
and Pelicans

For further information about books available from
Penguins please write to Dept EP, Penguin Books Ltd,
Harmondsworth, Middlesex UB7 0DA.

In the U.S.A.: For a complete list of books available
from Penguins in the United States write to Dept CS,
Penguin Books, 625 Madison Avenue, New York,
New York 10022.

In Canada: For a complete list of books available from
Penguins in Canada write to Penguin Books Canada Ltd,
2801 John Street, Markham, Ontario L3R 1B4.

In Australia: For a complete list of books available from
Penguins in Australia write to the Marketing Department,
Penguin Books Australia Ltd, P.O. Box 257, Ringwood,
Victoria 3134.

In New Zealand: For a complete list of books available
from Penguins in New Zealand write to the Marketing
Department, Penguin Books (N.Z.) Ltd, P.O. Box 4019,
Auckland 10.